Savitribai Phule

Celebrating
30 Years of Publishing
in India

Advance Praise for *Savitribai Phule*

'When you count the world's greatest champions of education, make sure to include Savitribai Phule in the list.'

—Andre Agassi, tennis champion and chairperson, Square Panda Foundation

'Savitribai Phule's work is foundational. She had courage and exemplary vision. She realized that without education, there could be no progress and persevered towards making it happen. She deserves to be embedded in our memory and public consciousness.'

—Raghunath Anant Mashelkar, former director-general, CSIR

'An excellent, equitable education will build India's next generation of leaders. The important work of Savitribai Phule and her companions in the nineteenth century is a bright colour in the canvas of India's history.'

—Shaheen Mistri, CEO, Teach For India

Also by Reeta Ramamurthy Gupta

Sanjeev Kumar: The Actor We All Loved (with Uday Jariwala)

Savitribai Phule

Her Life, Her Relationships, Her Legacy

REETA RAMAMURTHY GUPTA

HarperCollins *Publishers* India

First published in India by HarperCollins *Publishers* 2023
4th Floor, Tower A, Building No. 10, DLF Cyber City,
DLF Phase II, Gurugram, Haryana – 122002
www.harpercollins.co.in

2 4 6 8 10 9 7 5 3

P-ISBN: 978-93-5699-349-5
E-ISBN: 978-93-5699-350-1

The views and opinions expressed in this book are the author's own and the facts are as reported by her, and the publishers are not in any way liable for the same. A few characters in the book are fictional and have been added to enhance the narrative. They are true to their time and context and any resemblance to persons living or dead is wholly coincidental.

Typeset in 11.5/15.2 Bell MT Std at
Manipal Technologies Limited, Manipal

Printed and bound at
Replika Press Pvt. Ltd.

FSC
www.fsc.org
MIX
Paper from
responsible sources
FSC® C016779

This book is printed on FSC® certified paper
which ensures responsible forest management.

If you are an Indian woman who reads, you owe her.
If you are an educated Indian woman, you owe her.
If you are an Indian schoolgirl reading this chapter in English, you owe her.
If you are an educated international 'desi' woman, you owe her.[1]

—Thom Wolf and Suzana Andrade

1 Thom Wolf and Suzana Andrade, 'Savitribai and India's Conversation on Education', *Oikos Worldviews Journal*, 2008.

Contents

Section 3
Khandoji Nevse Patil

Section 4
A Revolution Takes Birth

PART 2
THE FIRE

Section 5
Sagunabai's Matchmaking Skills

Section 6
A Tale of Two Sisters

Foreword

We are all sons and daughters of Savitribai Phule, the great revolutionist of Maharashtra who gave us the gift of 'education for all'. Every educated Indian anywhere in the world, especially women, are beholden to Savitribai's venerable work in the field of education, dignity and social upliftment.

She helped the oppressed people to chart a dignified way of living. As these citizens started to read books and newspapers and got exposed to new ideas and concepts, they felt empowered and enriched.

Savitribai also worked for the prohibition of female infanticide, advocated widow remarriage and her beautiful poems awakened the vulnerable sections of society. Savitribai Phule's work addressed the structural inequities at the time. As more and more Indians followed her thoughts, their minds opened up to the ideas of freedom, justice and liberty. This catalysed the idea of nationhood.

—Devendra Fadnavis

Deputy Chief Minister of Maharashtra

A Frame of Reference

Stop for a moment. Consider how tenuous the liberty you enjoy today is. And how many sacrifices were made for you.

India was enslaved for centuries, not because others were strong, but because we were weak and disunited. 'In April 1836, there were just over 17,000 British troops in India of whom over a thousand were utterly unfit for duty and another 1400 were invalids, most the victims of venereal diseases or chronic alcoholism.'[1]

Looking over these figures, Governor-General Lord Auckland (1836–1842) commented that the Raj would face an unprecedented danger 'if ever the 80-millions of natives by whom they are surrounded by should be out of humour . . .'

1 Lawrence James, *Raj: The Making and Unmaking of British India* (St Martin's Press, 1997).

Thankfully, social reformers Jyotirao Phule and his wife Savitribai Phule were out of humour! They lived in nineteenth-century Poona, where society was rigidly built on the chaturvarna system comprising the Brahmins, Kshatriyas, Vaishyas and Shudras. The caste system was myopic and oppressive, and this was a dark period.

They fought against societal ills to ensure 'education for all' because social justice, freedom and equal opportunity cannot exist without it.

The British made the fatal error of supporting their efforts. They underestimated the impact of education on Indians and focused on the short-term goal of cheap labour to run their administration. The education of Indians became the nemesis of British arrogance and superiority. The spark lit by Jyotirao, Savitri and their friends and supporters fired the flame of nationhood as educated Indians grouped, coordinated, rebelled and eventually reclaimed independent India!

Setting the Context

Britain's relationship with India began with a sense of awe at her wealth and vast expanse. The British set up the East India Company, a monopolistic trading body, in 1600. Initially, the East India Company took little interest in the education of Indians. As traders, their interest lay in doing business and the majority of their interactions were with India's business class. This intermingling had another consequence—many Company officials and English military men married local Indian women. Reading through the wills of employees of the East India Company, one finds that in the 1780s, more than one-third of the British men in India left all their possessions to one or more Indian wives, or to their Anglo-Indian children.[2]

2 William Dalrymple, *White Mughals*, (Penguin Random House India, 2004).

History bears evidence that with time, Britain's relationship with India degenerated; the awe turned into greed, subjugation, disdain and even pity. To understand this transformation, let us train our lens on nineteenth-century British rule, a period notable for its 'surrogate emphasis' on education. Make no mistake, nothing can justify the plunder and loot that the British (or other rulers before them) were indulging in, not just in India but all over the world.

But here's the twist in the tale—Indian social reformers born in the British-ruled Maratha Confederacy in the nineteenth century did not see the British as their 'immediate' enemy. What disturbed them far more was the religious and social authority of the Brahmins. Young teen widows would be burnt on the same pyre after the death of their husbands (Sati) and child marriages were common (women were often married off to men five times their age). Polygamy, tonsuring of widows and female infanticide were rampant. This despotism was maintained by the Brahmins, thanks to their mental enslavement of society by breeding superstition and denying the right of education for all, especially women and the backward classes. So, the British thought, let us civilize the Indians a bit.

In 1813, a clause was inserted into the East India Company's charter to encourage missionary activity in India and to invest 10,000 pounds annually in education. In came the missionaries (including French, German and American missionaries), who preached 'social reconstruction with a moral revolution'. This seemed like manna from heaven for the social reformers, who were enraged by the 'liddism'[3] and oppression practised by the Brahmins.

3 A modern term that refers to the practice of 'putting a lid' on voices to suppress them.

Almost concurrently, the rise of the evangelical movement in England in the 1830s and 1840s put a brake on inter-religious marriages between British officers and Indian women. The evangelicals believed that the future prosperity of the British and the future happiness of the Indians themselves depended upon complete anglicization of Indian society. 'Let us endeavour to strike our roots into the soil,' said British reformer William Wilberforce,[4] 'by the gradual introduction and establishment of our own principles and opinions; of our laws, institutions, and manners; above all as the sources of every other improvement, of our religion, and consequently of our morals.'

Latter-day wills written by East India Company servants attest that the practice of marrying or cohabiting with Indian women had all but disappeared by the middle of the nineteenth century. The spread of their religion, however, was in full flow, with missionaries such as William Carey[5] proposing that 'faith alone is enough for membership to the Christian community'.

The missionaries discovered with time that a majority of Indian social reformers wanted education but not religious conversion. So, the British Empire embarked upon a 'civilization mission'. They wanted social and cultural transformation, to which education was central.

---

4 William Wilberforce (1759–1833) was a British politician and philanthropist who, from 1787, was prominent in the struggle to abolish the slave trade and then to abolish slavery itself in British overseas possessions.

5 William Carey (1761–1834) was an English Christian missionary who founded the Serampore College and the Serampore University, the first degree-awarding university in India.

In the hundred years[6] from the Battle of Plassey in 1757 to the uprising of 1857, the East India Company began to function more as an administrator and less as a trading concern. But India was such a vast country that it became increasingly apparent to the British that they didn't have enough manpower to administer the country. Hence, it became necessary to hire Indians at lower levels in the administrative machinery. To do this, they had to educate the Indians, make them conversant in English.

However, Lord Cornwallis, who established the civil service in British India, believed that 'every native of Hindoostan is corrupt'. Hence, the British did not really trust the Indians to hold high positions in the civil service.

The Indian education system at the time was not suited to the needs of the British administrative service. A report in 1830 by William Adams[7] about the education system in Bengal stated that there were temple pathshalas that taught Hindi and Sanskrit, Muslim maktabs that taught Urdu, Persian and Arabic, and gurdwaras that taught Gurmukhi and Punjabi.

The Brahmins taught the Vedas and shastras in their schools (temple pathshalas), which served their own purpose. Both Indian reformers, who wanted progress, and Christian missionaries, who wanted to propagate the ideals of Christianity, believed that modern education would be the key to making things happen.

But what really changed was that the British wanted India to be educated for their own reasons. It was in July 1833 that Lord

6 The Battle of Plassey signifies the beginning of British rule in India. A hundred years later, the uprising of 1857 was one of the earliest revolts that challenged this British rule.

7 Refer to Annexure 2 for an extract from Part 1 of William Adam's report to get a sense of what kind of education Fatima Sheikh, a key character in our story, might have received.

Macaulay[8] stated, while defending the East India Company's Charter Bill of 1813 on behalf of the government, 'The mere extent of Empire is not necessarily an advantage. To many Governments, it has been cumbersome. [...] Far better for us that the people of India were well-governed and independent of us, than ill-governed and subject to us.'

William Bentinck, who became the governor-general of India in 1833, understood the problem and sought to liberate Indian subjects from the despotism of Brahmins. In 1835 the then Government of India (the British Empire) decided that the teaching of Western sciences and literature would happen through the English language alone. Lord Macaulay, a British parliamentarian, believed that Indian languages were not sufficiently developed to serve the purpose of Western scientific education.

Reformers such as Raja Ram Mohan Roy also advocated the study of Western knowledge because traditional education was breeding superstition, fear and authoritarianism, and Western education held 'the key to the treasures of scientific and democratic thought of the modern West'. Lord Macaulay elaborated further, 'We must at present do our best to form a class who may be interpreters between us and the millions whom we govern; a class of persons Indians in blood and colour, but English in taste, in opinion, in morals and in intellect.' And herein lies the paradox.

8 On 10 June 1834, Lord Macaulay arrived in India as a lawyer serving on the Governor-General's Executive Council and was chosen to lead the Committee of Public Instruction. On 2 February 1835, he circulated a 'Minute on Education', which was a treatise that offered definitive reasons for why the East India Company and the British government should spend money on the provision of English language education, especially the sciences, in India.

The British maintained that they had limited budgets to open institutes of higher education. So, they adopted the famous downward filtration theory.[9] This theory assumed that teaching a handful of Indians from the upper and middle classes would help them, in turn, teach the masses. To the chagrin and dismay of all, the education did not percolate down. The Brahmins cannibalized most of these institutions and since they were the teachers, they did not allow the lower classes to enter. Pressed by manpower issues, the British further made an official announcement in 1844, under Governor-General Lord Hardinge,[10] that all applicants for government jobs should know English. This declaration made English-medium schools very popular and compelled more and more students to abandon traditional schools.

The British had a huge motive—to economize the cost of running India. It was becoming too expensive to maintain a large number of Britishers in India for the administration of the country. You see, there was never any master plan for India in their minds. They just took a series of tactical decisions one after another in response to local and unexpected crises.[11]

The paradox, therefore, was this: the period from 1844 to 1854 was a particularly foggy one—the British wanted to educate the masses but were not prepared to invest money. The Brahmins were not willing to let go of their hold over education, and they stood as blockades, as self-appointed custodians of learning,

---

9 In 1835 Lord Macaulay was also responsible for the Downward Filtration Theory in his famous 'Macaulay's Minutes'.

10 Henry Hardinge, a British soldier and statesman, was governor-general of India from 1844 to 1848.

11 Lawrence James, *Raj: The Making and Unmaking of British India*, (St Martin's Press, 1997).

monopolizing all the incentives and jobs that the British were offering. Women and the lower castes had no access to education. The British responded to this by supporting missionaries, associations, social reformers, etc.; anyone who would help the cause of education.

It was in this critical tug-of-war that Savitribai Phule found her voice. She and her husband, Jyotirao Phule, lived in Poona, a part of the Maratha Confederacy, a traditional Brahmin stronghold. The couple and their band of bravehearts set up eighteen schools for girls and the downtrodden.

Key Dates

1773: The Regulating Act is passed, and the British Government takes greater interest in the territorial affairs of the East India Company

1784: The India Act is passed, and the British Government takes control over the East India Company's affairs and its administration in India

1792: William Carey promotes the Baptist Missionary Society (BMS) in England—marking the beginning of the modern foreign missionary movement in the English-speaking world—and becomes its first missionary to India in 1793. He also publishes a pamphlet titled 'An Enquiry into the Obligations of Christians'. He makes the point that 'poor, barbarous naked pagans [referring to Indians] are exactly as capable of education as we are'

1813: The Charter Act establishes the Crown's undoubted sovereignty over all the Company's territories and requires it to open up India to Christian missionaries

1827: Birth of Jyotirao Phule
1831: Birth of Savitri Patil
1831: Birth of Fatima Sheikh
1833: The Government of India Act of 1833 restructures the governance of the country. It states that no native of India should be disabled from holding any place, office or employment due to religion
1835: The government decides to teach Western sciences in English alone
1840: Savitri and Jyotirao get married
1844: The British Government declares that applicants for government jobs should possess knowledge of English
1847: Savitri becomes a qualified teacher
1848: Jyotirao and Savitri set up the first school for girls at Bhidewada.
1849: Savitri and Jyotirao are asked to leave home by Jyotirao's father Govindrao.
1852: Govindrao, Jyotirao's father, dies
1852: Savitri Phule starts the Mahila Seva Mandal
1853: Savitri Phule establishes the first-ever infanticide prohibition home in India
1854: Savitri Phule champions the cause of widow remarriage and starts a home for lower- and upper-caste widows
1856: Fatima Sheikh gets married
1857: The mutiny against the British takes place
1858: The Government of India Act of 1858 transfers the government and territories of the East India Company to the British Crown.
1862: Death of Cynthia Farrar
1874: The East India Company is formally dissolved by an act of Parliament
1890: Death of Jyotirao Phule
1897: Death of Savitri Phule

'Chaturvarnya would have been a very innocent principle if it meant no more than mere division of society into four classes.

Unfortunately, more than this is involved in the theory of chaturvarnya. Besides dividing society into four orders, the theory goes further and makes the principle of graded inequality.'

—B.R. Ambedkar[12]

12 This quote is from *Who Were the Shudras?*, a history book published by Indian social reformer and polymath B.R. Ambedkar in 1946. The book discusses the origin of the Shudra varna. Ambedkar dedicated the book to Jyotirao Phule, whom he considered his mentor.

Prologue

Long before the young and feisty Malala Yousafzai became a Nobel laureate and a voice for the education of oppressed women, there was Savitribai Phule, one of the world's greatest teachers, who fought tirelessly for the education of women and the lower castes of India.

Fatima Sheikh, almost forgotten by history, was a committed aide-de-camp, wing woman and friend to her mentor Savitri. Born in nineteenth-century India, in modern-day Uttar Pradesh, Fatima learnt Urdu, Arabic, Marathi and English. Whether she was the first female Muslim teacher of India or the first female headmistress of India is inconsequential. What is known and accepted is that Fatima's work to ensure women's education and social unshackling, alongside her better-known collaborator Savitri, reverberates around India and the world.

This unique friendship has been forgotten by history. In fact, if not for the photograph[13] that is available in M.G. Mali's seminal book on Savitribai Phule, titled *Krantijyoti Savitribai Jyotirao Phule*, my journey to find out more about Fatima Sheikh and Sagunabai Kshirsagar would never have started.

I also found a letter, attributed to Savitri Phule, written on 10 October 1856, specifically mentioning Fatima Sheikh.[14] At the time, Savitri was unwell and had gone to stay for a prolonged undocumented period with her parents in Naigaon. The task of running the schools they had set up at the time was left to Fatima. In the letter she wrote, 'I will come to Poona as soon as I have completely recovered. Please don't be worried about me.

---

13 There is a picture in *Kratijyoti Savitribai Jyotirao Phule* by M.G. Mali (Majestic Publishing House, 1980) labelled 'Savitribai Phule and Fatima Sheikh with two students from their school'. In that picture, beside Savitribai is seated another woman, while a third woman is standing behind them, dressed in white clothes. According to historian Dr Ganesh Raut, this third woman could be Saguna Kshirsagar. But where is the proof that this picture is authentic?

Fortunately, Dr Mali has written a note below the photograph (developed from a negative that is over a hundred years old). The source of this picture dates back to Savitribai's photograph printed in *Majur*, a paper published from Pune many years ago—somewhere between 1924 and 1930. R.N. Lad was the editor of the paper at the time. D.S. Jogde also worked as the editor for some time. Dr Mali got this picture from D.S. Jogde.

According to Dr Mali, 'A rare photograph was printed in the famous book written by a missionary named Lokande. That photograph and the picture printed in *Majur* look identical. Savitribai's picture was painted on the basis of the photograph. Eknath Palkar of Pune too had some negatives. Jogde got this negative from Palkar. From that negative, the pictures of Savitribai Phule and Fathima Shaikh became available.'

14 Susie Tharu and K. Lalita, eds, *Women Writing in India: 600 BC to the Present*, Vol. 1, (The Feminist Press, 1991).

This must be causing a lot of trouble to Fatima. But I am sure she will understand and won't grumble.'

Likewise, limited histories are available for the enterprising teacher Sagunabai Kshirsagar, the adoptive mother to Jyotirao Phule and Saraswati Govande, whose contribution was pivotal to setting up the mahila seva mandal. As I dug deeper, met countless scholars, notably historians Dr Ganesh Raut, Prof. Hari Narke, Dr Shamshuddin Tamboli, educationist Dr Benazeer Tamboli, social activist Baba Adhav, and translated several Marathi texts, I found scant and scattered references to them, all of which are indexed in this book. Now, history tends to remember those who leave plenty of evidence of their work. Unfortunately, none of them wrote or published articles and books, unlike Jyotirao or Savitribai. Neither are there diaries or other tracks available.

As a woman and a writer, I owe the entirety of my work to Savitribai Phule. And if you are a woman reading this book, so do you. Far beyond the ideas of caste, creed and individual differences, she and her 'sisters in arms' believed that one's birth must not determine one's destiny.

Our book spans the four decades from 1818—the end of Peshwai[15]—to 1856, the year after which records of Sagunabai Kshirsagar, Saraswati Govande and Fatima Sheikh are no longer available.

And then some …

15 A local Marathi way of referring to the rule of the peshwas.

Jyotirao Phule's name is not on the cover of this book, but his spirit is imbued in it. He has rightly been called the Father of India's Social Revolution and a 'Mahatma' by no less than Mahatma Gandhi himself. He was the conscience keeper and spokesman of the nameless, faceless oppressed millions of India in the nineteenth century.

No wonder, then, that Dr B.R. Ambedkar regarded him as one of his three gurus (the other two being the Buddha and Kabir), which is proof enough of his invaluable historical legacy. All through his life Phule fought against every form of servitude and infused a new spirit in the subjugated masses.

Facing page: (*Left to right*) Fatima Sheikh and Savitribai Phule with Saguna Kshirsagar and two children from their school seated in front. Reproduced with permission from Majestic Publishers.

सावित्रीबाई फुले आणि फातिमा शेख त्यांच्या
शाळेतील दोन विद्यार्थिनींसह
(शंभर वर्षांपूर्वी निगेटिव्हवरून तयार केलेले दुर्मिळ छायाचित्र)

PART 1

THE SPARK

Section 1

Not So Long Ago …

Among Savitribai's various collaborators, the most information is available about Fatima Sheikh. Here's her story in brief.

Fatima's family migrated from Uttar Pradesh to Maharashtra[1] and settled in Malegaon (present-day Nashik district). Her family members were handloom textile merchants. When Fatima was barely seven years old, the family moved to Poona from Malegaon owing to the crisis that arose in the handloom textile business and a drought that hit the region. When her parents died early, her brother, Usman Sheikh Pinjara, became her guardian. The young siblings settled in the Ganzpet area in Poona city, and Munshi[2] Gafar

---

1 The term 'Maharashtra', wherever it is used in the book, loosely suggests the region of western India that was broadly Marathi-speaking; it is not intended to necessarily indicate the wider areas covered by present-day Maharashtra. In actuality, Maharashtra did not constitute a single administrative unit during the nineteenth century. It was divided into the Bombay Presidency, Hyderabad, Central Provinces and Berar. Poona (now Pune) and Bombay (now Mumbai) were the two main centres of intellectual fermentation during the period, and they, thus, prominently figured in the discourse.

2 Munshi is not a name but a profession and refers to someone who is a scribe and interpreter of official correspondence, as well as a teacher of Persian.

Baig (Baig Sahab), an Urdu and Persian scholar, stood as a father figure to them.

Over time, Usman became a successful trader. With her brother being in the garment trade, Fatima learnt kashidakari (embroidery) and tailoring, and taught young girls in her house. She met Savitri Phule at Mrs Mitchell's school in Poona, where they both took lessons in English. Savitri had never met anyone like Fatima, a very well-read girl in her own right. She could quote Urdu poetry at will and was an avid reader of Persian. They formed a unique friendship, and Fatima supported the implementation of Savitri's fiery crusade to change the lot of girls and women in society.

Scholar Dr Shamsuddin Tamboli and author Dinakar Vishnu Kakade believe that Fatima Sheikh got married; Jyoti and Savitri gave her hand away in marriage. Following her marriage, Fatima left Poona and the details of her life after marriage aren't available. However, we have considered a possible course she might have taken.

1
Flash Forward

We open our story in the year 1888. Mahatma Jyotirao Phule had recently suffered a stroke and was rendered paralysed in his right hand. Despite many requests by everyone to rest, he would prop himself up and write with his left hand.

A poor Brahmin lady lived with the couple for cleaning, washing dishes, sweeping and cooking. They paid her, even though they did not have much money. There was a pile of slates, chalk and books in one corner of the living room, neatly arranged—whenever a child would visit, he or she would take one. Govind Ganapat Kale,[3] a friend's son, also lived with them as an accountant and help.

3 A lot of context is provided in Govind Ganpat Kale's essay in the book *Amhi Pahilele Phule*, a compilation of recollections narrated by Jyotirao Phule's associates and contemporaries, compiled by Pandharinath Patil and edited by Sitaram Raikar, (Mahatma Jyotirao Phule Samata Pratisthan, 1981).

Dr Vishram Ramji Ghollay had just visited Jyotirao.

Jyotirao spoke with effort, even though he already knew the answer to the question, 'Savitri, did Ghollay take any money?'

Savitri shook her head.

'Why doesn't he take his fees from us? How will he survive?' asked Jyoti with some consternation.

Ghollay was a renowned doctor in Poona at that time, but he did not charge Jyotirao a single rupee for the medicines and his treatment. He would say, 'Just give me the privilege of a cup of tea.'

After the doctor left, Savitri was folding clothes and sitting next to Jyotirao. Her entire day was spent taking care of her husband. She had referred to him as Shetji since the day of their wedding. Jyoti had a bad cough, which was why Savitri had called the doctor. But there was no dimming the light in his eyes.

Just then, a visitor was announced. Both of them were happy to see Govind Babaji.[4] Babaji[5] was very close to the Maharaja of Baroda Shrimant Sayajirao Gaekwad.[6] Babaji was a pioneer when it came to advocating intermarriage among castes and a huge admirer of Jyotirao's work. When Babaji saw the condition of Jyotirao's health, he was aghast.

'Jyotiba, you look very frail.'

Jyoti smiled. 'I am an old man now, Babaji! Has age ever spared anyone? Besides, nobody lets me do anything. Kale here takes care of the farms and all the accounts. Sasane takes care of

4 A reference to this meeting is given in N.K. Wagle (ed.), *Writers, Editors and Reformers*, (Manohar Books, 1999).

5 Govind Babaji Joshi was the first Hindu missionary in Maharashtra. A reformer by thought, he was a public speaker in the service of the Maharaja of Baroda.

6 'Govindrav Babaji Joshi Goes to Madras' in N.K. Wagle, *A 'Diary' of the Third Indian National Congress* (Routledge, 1991).

the vegetable shops and food distribution camps. Lokhande has taken over my task of educating mill workers and making them aware of their rights.'

Babaji looked almost apologetic as he said, 'Sayajirao sends his regards. He has also sent one thousand rupees for your expenses. He misses your visits to the palace in Baroda.'

Jyotirao shook his head, then smiled. 'Babaji, all money is welcome. I have always known that nothing can be achieved without money. That is why I became a contractor in my younger days and worked for the British.[7] Please thank Sayajirao; tell him that only my right hand is paralysed. My mind is alert, and I still have a lot of work to do.'

Kale came forward to take the money. 'I will deposit this in the Satyashodhak Samaj fund,' he said. Savitri nodded as the maid brought tea for everyone.

Babaji spoke slowly and deliberately, 'You must rest, Jyotiba.'

Savitri laughed. 'Shetji and rest? He still wakes up at 4 a.m. every day. By 5 a.m., he goes for a walk to Parvati hill. He meets his usual friends on the way. Then he comes home, has a bath, eats roasted bhakri[8] in milk. Then, he starts writing with his left hand.[9] Sometimes, in the mornings, he sits outside the house. Those days, the stream of visitors is never-ending!'

---

7 Jyotirao Phule was a successful contractor. He won a contract for the Katraj tunnel on the Poona–Satara road. Apart from this, he had taken a contract to provide stones and lime for the construction of the Mula-Mutha dam and the Yerwada bridge. The construction of barracks and digging of pipes under the Mula-Mutha dam were done by Jyotirao himself. He used the profits from these contract works to support his social work.

8 A type of flatbread made of jowar or bajra.

9 Many such conversations have been created with the input of eminent historian Dr Ganesh Raut.

Jyotirao spoke in an even tone, mellowed with age. 'Savitri, people come to us because they have problems. Sometimes, I feel that before one problem is solved, another one presents itself. When we were fighting for the education of the girl child, Shudras, Mahars and Mangs, the Brahmins were the enemy. The Britishers helped us. Now, it seems that the British are the enemy. British collectors, magistrates and judges are sitting in their airy offices and bungalows. They couldn't care less about the plight of the Kunbi cultivators and their extortion by the zamindars and moneylenders.'

Babaji nodded slowly. 'Yes. But didn't you tell this to Duke Sahab[10] when he came?'

Savitri shook her head in despair. 'Babaji, that function was such a farce! You should've seen in what shringar the guests showed up! Silks, diamond necklaces and jewels all over! Shetji was shocked because he went dressed as a farmer.'

Jyotirao had a mischievous glint in his eye. 'Arre Savitri, my name is Phule, I grow flowers, and I am a Mali. That's why I dressed like a farmer. I told Hari Raoji Chiplunkar, who arranged the function, that I was going to be honest with Duke Sahab. Everyone showed up like it was a wedding. Their fanfare did not represent reality, it was very misleading. If the Duke of Connaught is really interested in learning about the condition of the subjects of the Queen, he should take the trouble to visit some villages as well as the areas in the city occupied by the untouchables. I told him as much!'

Babaji laughed. Jyotirao's honesty had always been his biggest strength. He never minced words.

10 On 2 March 1888, Hari Raoji Chiplunkar, a friend of Jyotirao, arranged a function in honour of the Duke and Duchess of Connaught.

Jyoti continued, 'Babaji, that was one of the most frustrating days of my life. God knows I have had many such days. Because often, my work does not have the desired effect. Nothing changed, even when I sent copies of my book *The Cultivator's Whip*[11] to Lord Lytton. Are the Kunbi[12] farmers any better off today?'

Jyotirao was clearly disturbed. His voice was now trembling. Savitri patted his hand and asked him to calm down.

Feeling a twinge of sympathy for Jyotirao, Babaji said, 'Jyotiba, you cannot solve all the problems of the world in one day.'

Hoping to change the topic, after a moment of silence, Babaji asked, 'Whose photograph is this?'

He was referring to a photograph of Savitribai and two other women.

Jyotirao's worried face broke into a wide smile. 'Savitri, see, Fatima and Saguna Aau also want to be part of this conversation.'

Babaji asked with a quizzical expression, 'Who are they?'

Savitri spoke warmly, 'Saguna Aau was our guiding light. Fatima was my closest friend, my most dependable ally in our success with the education of girls. She was a very courageous woman. We lost touch. I last saw her at Cynthia Farrar's funeral.'

'Cynthia Farrar, your teacher in Ahmednagar?'

Savitri nodded.

---

11 'Shetkaryache asud' or 'cultivator's whipcord' is a wonderful metaphor invented by Mahatma Jyotirao Phule. He wrote a book by that name in 1881 in which he expressed the view that the whip a farmer carries to control his livestock should not be limited to this purpose. Rather, he felt that it should be used to overcome all the injustice the farmer faces. It was the strongest weapon in the hands of farmers to fight exploitation, to pursue truth and to oppose the wicked.

12 Kunbi (alternatively Kanbi) is a generic term applied to castes of traditionally non-elite farmers in western India. These include the Dhonoje, Ghatole, Hindre, Jadav, Jhare, Khaire, Lewa (Leva Patil), Lonare and Tirole communities of Vidarbha.

Jyotirao looked happy again. 'You know, Fatima taught Savitri and me how to ignore criticism. She would always quote Mohammad Paigambar, the founder of Islam, "*Tum dharti waalon par daya karo, aakashwala (Allah) tum par daya karega.*"[13] All my life, that is all I have done. Criticism never bothered me because I knew I was fighting for those who couldn't fight for themselves.'

Savitri chimed in, 'Fatima had a favourite line to tell all the parents who were stubborn about not educating their daughters and unwilling to change their ways:

Jo sarkash raha, woh fanaa hua
Jo thoda jhuk gaya, wahi sab paa gaya!
(Those who are stubborn have to sacrifice themselves
Those who bend a little, receive all blessings)

'It was something she wrote on her own. Fatima was such a fine poet. When I published *Kavya Phule* in 1854, I insisted that she publish a book of her poems too. She had immense knowledge of Persian and Urdu and composed many poems. Sadly, she never published. Neither did Saguna Aau. Now, other than this photograph, we have nothing of theirs.'

Babaji remarked, 'I don't think history will forget your work, or that of Fatima Sheikh and Saguna Aau. We will not let them forget.'

---

13 Be kind to those on earth, God will be kind to you.

2

The Agra Presidency, 1837

In the Agra Presidency,[14] a seven-year-old girl named Fatima was sitting in her house, pretending to be busy embroidering a dupatta as her abba entered, looking dejected. She didn't want to meet his gaze. She knew something was wrong; Ammi hadn't made sheer-kurma in the longest time!

Abba gestured to Ammi to join him, then shut the door to their room. Fatima had realized that increasingly, her parents were having conversations that they didn't want her to hear. As soon as the door closed, Fatima leapt up with the stealth of a hunter and pressed her ear to the door. Her father was informing her mother about their move to Maliwadi (Malegaon).

14 The Presidency of Agra was established on 14 November 1834 under the provisions of the Government of India Act, 1833, by elevating and renaming the Ceded and Conquered Provinces, a region in northern India that was ruled by the British East India Company from 1805 to 1834.

'Where is that?' her mother exclaimed.

Fatima wondered too. Malegaon sounded very far away. And what would they do there? It was all very unsettling.

Fatima's family belonged to the Julaha community. The Julahas were weavers and their craftsmanship had always been a matter of pride. However, their trade had been badly impacted by the famine.[15] Peer Sahab, the local soothsayer, had prophesied that the summer rains would fail and so would the kharif crop.

Abba continued, 'It is a long journey by road, but we have no choice. There is some talk that the British have started cutting off the thumbs of the weavers in Bengal and that it might happen here too.'

Fatima let it all sink in. Cut off thumbs? Could they do that? And yes, she had heard Fazal Chacha talk about the qahat, the famine, when he had visited the previous evening.

'These Britishers have made us beggars in our own lands.' Abba broke down completely. Fatima could hear him sob.

'But where will we stay?' Ammi asked gently.

Fatima liked how Ammi always got straight to the point.

'Thankfully, that's the silver lining. Ali has received word that many Julahas are settling in Malegaon, building a community. His great-grandfather went there to build a fort for Naro Shankar.[16] Ali told me that there are two rivers in Malegaon,

---

15 The Agra famine of 1837–1838 refers to the famine in the Northwestern Provinces of Company-ruled India that affected an area of 25,000 square miles and a population of 8 million people.

16 A large number of Muslims settled in Malegaon post 1740, when a local jagirdar, Naro Shankar Raje Bahadur, started building the Malegaon Fort. Muslim workers came from the northern parts of India as well as Surat during the construction period, which spanned twenty-five years. The British conquered the fort in 1818, following which it became a refuge for Muslims from all over India, persecuted by famine or political unrest.

Girna and Mausam, fertile land and plenty of water. It is perfect for weavers,' Abba declared.

Fatima could almost hear her mother's heart sink. Then she heard her father walk towards the door. Fatima rushed back to her seat and continued with her embroidery. What troubled her was that she did not understand what rivers had to do with moving. Wasn't there a river where they lived too? And yet, it seemed that they had to move.

Just then, her brother Usman entered the house. He had a calm, Zen-like demeanour. Just the person she wanted to see. She jumped up, pulled him by the hand, took him to the courtyard outside and blurted out everything she had heard.

All of eleven, Usman was mature for his age. He had seen his father work hard and yet not receive due respect. The Julahas were identified as a low caste. Their self-image as a community was not only affected by other high-caste Muslims, but also by how they were treated by the British. The Julahas therefore had no choice but to stick together. Usman knew that their upcoming move was a planned collective exodus, thanks to a kin connection.

He could see that Fatima was very upset.

Fatima said indignantly, 'Bhaijaan, I don't want to go to Malegaon.'

Usman knew they had no choice. 'Our community is not valued here, Fatima. It will probably be the same there as well. So what difference does it make where we live?'

Muslims were divided into the ashraf—the nobility, aristocracy, scholars, etc.; and the ajlaf—the lower class comprising traders and artisans, which was the lot of Fatima's family. The ashraf class was used to being wooed by the British, at least for a while. The ajlaf—they did not exist and were dispensable, at least some of them.

Fatima, in her innocence, did not share Usman's despondency. 'What are you talking about? Of course it makes a difference. My new teacher is going to come home from tomorrow.'

Usman smiled. Fatima was so bright that in the maktab, she had memorized the Quran. She was brighter than most boys he knew. And yet, her innocence was untouched by reality.

Usman knew he had to be firm. 'Do you even know what is happening outside the house, Fatima? People like our father do not even have the right to name their own children anymore. They are in debt to the zamindars due to the famine. Fazal Chacha's neighbour's son was recently named "Gadha" (donkey) by his zamindar.'

Fatima was aghast. She knew none of this. Usman realized that he had scared her. He added soothingly, 'It's not just Abba. All of his weaver friends are going too. So we will all be together—just in another place where there is no famine.'

Fatima was crestfallen. She really wanted to study more and had pestered her parents to find her a tutor.

Just then, the brother-sister duo was summoned. As they turned to go inside, the evening was turning to night.

Anguished chants of 'Ya-Hussain', 'Hasan' and 'Haider' started filling the air, at first from a distance. Then the sounds of cymbals and drums became louder and louder. Fatima and Usman watched as a long procession of barefooted, bare-chested men clad in black approached. They were carrying tazias and taboots and rhythmically beating their chests till they bled. Some screamed out their lamentations and then fainted in an ecstasy of sorrow.

Muharram had begun. Mourning had begun.

Within a week, Fatima's family started their journey to Malegaon.

3

The Long Journey to Malegaon

The move to Malegaon was something of a mass exodus for the Julaha community of weavers. Many of them wanted to make a fresh beginning away from both the famine and the atrocities of the British; a few of them also harboured the desire to gain an equal standing in the fraternity of Islam. Some of them did not believe that this was possible.

The arduous travel took its toll on Fatima's mother. This was before the age of railways, so Fatima's family travelled by bullock cart. The journey took over five days. The long, difficult journey of over a thousand kilometres was interrupted by rain, sun and the odd storm. Protecting her children with all her might, Fatima's mother reached Malegaon critically ill and soon breathed her last. The brutality of the journey, the loss of his livelihood and the death of his wife consumed Fatima's father. With no will to live, he too passed away a couple of years later.

Usman had just turned thirteen at the time. He was determined to overcome his penury and build something meaningful. He was painfully aware that his unmarried sister was attracting all kinds of attention.

Educationist Dr Benazeer Tamboli[17] suggests that the alliance that their father had fixed for Fatima in the Agra Presidency might have become null and void. Perhaps the famine had changed social identities and some families responded by reneging on promises. Now, as orphans, Usman didn't have the resources to get Fatima married into a good family. Besides, those who agreed to marry her were of advanced age; Usman didn't want to spoil Fatima's future.

Usman taught Fatima kashidakari and tailoring. He kept her busy and dismissed the thought of his own marriage. Bringing in a wife would alter the balance of power in the household and Fatima might be at the losing end. Their neighbours offered supportive guardianship. Khadija Bi in particular was very supportive because Fatima took excellent care of her child, Rehana. Fatima's intelligence and perseverance were a huge support to Usman. Together, the two of them developed their skills and their reputation grew. However, fate struck another blow.

In 1842, the twin scares of drought and locusts[18] made living in Malegaon next to impossible. The siblings had to move again. Fatima and Usman went to Ganzpet in Poona. They travelled with Khadija Bi's family—her husband Fazal Chacha, their two-year-old son Abbas (whose name had been changed from Gadha!) and five-year-old daughter Rehana.

---

17 Author's conversation

18 Rustom Dinshaw Choksey, *Economic History of the Bombay Deccan and Karnatak (1818-1868)*, (University of Michigan, 1945).

The two families found themselves at the doorstep of Persian scholar Munshi Gafar Baig.[19] Something about the manner in which fifteen-year-old Usman was protecting eleven-year-old Fatima melted Baig Sahab's heart. He arranged for the two families to stay near his home.

Baig Sahab became a mentor and guide to the orphaned siblings. He introduced Usman to several influential people in Poona, and over the years, Usman became a successful trader.

Fazal Chacha, who had fallen sick in Malegaon, did not long survive the journey to Poona. He passed away, leaving Khadija and the kids to Usman's care.

Since the children were young, Usman immediately offered to employ Khadija Bi in his trading concern. Usman needed all the hands he could get to build a business, and he knew that Khadija Bi had too much at stake to be dishonest with him.

Fatima too began to teach young girls embroidery and tailoring in the house. As she grew into a teenager, Fatima's pleasant countenance and sunny outlook to life made her a favourite with British memsahibs, who offered their patronage to her embroidered shawls. Usman realized that Fatima was an asset and taught her basic mathematics so she could keep her own accounts.

Suffice it to say that Fatima was one of the most accomplished and intellectually empowered young women of her time. Regretfully, all she saw around her were teenage widows and abandoned wives. She was extremely grateful to her brother for sparing her the horror of a conventional existence.

---

19 Divya Kandukuri, 'The Life and Times of Savitribai Phule', *Mint*, 12 January 2019.

'The chief cause of India's ruin has been the monopolizing of the whole education and intelligence of the land by dint of pride and royal authority, among a handful of men . . . Where, except in India, can be had millions of men who will cut the throats of their own fathers and brothers for 6 rupees?'[20]

—Swami Vivekananda

20 Swami Vivekananda (1863–1902), in a letter to Sarala Ghoshal, editor of *Bharati*, dated 24 April 1897 (translated from Bengali), in Swami Vivekananda, *Reflections*, (Om Books, 2018).

Section 2

Poona, After Peshwai

We know that Fatima and Usman settled in Poona in 1842. Under the social structure of Poona at the time, the Brahmins ruled supreme. They wrote and taught texts that would give them the highest rights, the highest privileges and gifts, and everything that would make their lives easy, smooth and happy. On the other hand, the Shudras and Atishudras were regarded with hatred and contempt, and even basic human rights were denied to them.

The Prabhus and Brahmins of those days styled themselves as lords of the universe, even equal to God himself. They performed the unpardonable task of misinterpreting Hinduism with a view to oppress people.

4

The Bewildering Brahmins of Poona

Walk with me into the nineteenth-century Maratha Confederacy. Peshwai (a local term for Peshwa rule) was over by 1818. But the hangover remained. Brahmins, who had entrenched themselves in powerful positions in the Peshwai governance, continued to dictate social conduct even as the British consolidated their rule.

Society was built on the chaturvarna caste system comprising the Brahmins, Kshatriyas, Vaishyas and Shudras. Lower than the Shudras were the Atishudras, and both were mistreated in many ways.

The Brahmins considered it bad luck if they came across a Shudra in the morning. Hence, the Shudras were only allowed to come out of their homes at prescribed times.

The footprints of the Shudras on the road couldn't be seen by Brahmins. The soil contaminated by their passage had to be covered by another layer of soil, so they were forced to tie small tahalya (branches) to their waist with which they would sweep the path behind them as they walked. Further, a pot was tied to their necks so their saliva wouldn't drop on the road. They also had to tie a black thread around their necks so that they could be identified readily.

If a Shudra came across a Brahmin, they had to quickly sit down so their impure shadow wouldn't fall on the Brahmin. Shudras also had to carry a bell with them while walking on the street to forewarn others of higher caste and give the latter a chance to change their path.

The state of women was worse.

Birth as a woman meant a miserable existence. A man was allowed any number of marriages and that too with younger girls. At the age of sixty, Bajirao Peshwa II, the thirteenth and last Maratha ruler, married a girl who was only nine or ten years old. Needless to say, these girls would get widowed early. Their heads were then shaved, and they were forced to lead an ascetic life.

Funnily enough, the restrictions on women conferred a pious and reputable status to the family. Women were expected to stay behind the purdah, not come in front of men, laugh or talk loudly, or even wear footwear in front of men.

Women's education was considered to be against dharma.

There were reports that women from the lower castes were forced to dance for Brahmin men and their status was pronounced as worse than animals.

Widows would get raped. They would then be shamed into suicide.

Can you believe that this was our world less than two hundred years ago?

The story of Savitribai Phule is set in this time. And that is why it is important.

'The Englishman in India is proud and tenacious. He feels himself a conqueror amongst a vanquished people and looks down with some degree of superiority on all below him.'

—Henry Robertclaw, a young officer in the Company's judicial service (1805)

5

Governance after the Peshwas

James Mill's office, London 1819

James Mill was in deep thought. He had recently published three volumes titled *The History of British India.*[21] He abhorred Hindus and their denial of education to their fellow beings. His reverie was broken as his friend Jeremy Bentham was announced.

The two men had known each other for a decade. Bentham, a wealthy aristocrat, was twenty-five years older than Mill and believed that 'the object of all legislation must be the greatest happiness of the greatest number of people'. Now, whether the people were ready to receive this happiness remained a question.

21 James Mill, *The History of British India* in three volumes, (London: Baldwin, Cradock and Joy, 1817).

Thanks to their age difference, Bentham indulged Mill and was supportive of him.

Mill had come up the hard way. His father, James Milne, was a shoemaker and small farmer of modest means. His mother, Isabel Fenton Milne, was a more forceful figure. She changed the family name from the Scottish 'Milne' to the more English-sounding 'Mill' and kept young James away from other children, demanding that he spend most of his waking hours immersed in study.[22] He studied for the Ministry and eventually ended up in London in 1802, working as an independent author, journalist and editor.

Mill's hard work paid off when in 1819 he was appointed assistant examiner of correspondence at the East India Company.

In poorer times, Mill had befriended Jeremy Bentham because of the latter's wealth.

As Bentham entered, Mill envied the class that he exuded, even at his most casual. Bentham asked affably, 'How are Harriet and the children?'

This wasn't a casual question because James Mill had nine children!

Mill retorted, clutching his head with his hands, 'Is that the question you want to begin with?'

The two men laughed.

Bentham continued, 'Responsibilities, young man. They make us do boring things. Your books, for instance!'

Ten years into the friendship, Mill was getting tired of Bentham's jibes and wished that he would stop coming over as often as he did. This was a relationship that no longer served Mill.

Mill spoke sharply, 'You have no wife and no need to work! At best, you're a closet philosopher whose only outlet is to share

22 'James Mill', *Stanford Encyclopedia of Philosophy*, 27 November 2020

ideas over a drink with anyone who will listen. What you find boring today will be reference material tomorrow.'

Bentham wondered if his friend was insulting him or whether he should let it go. He chose the latter. 'Why are you in such a foul mood today?'

Just then, an usher entered with tea. The distraction diffused the situation.

Mill would often assert that he had earned his way in life, while Bentham was born into his position. Bentham was aware of his resentment, but he had a more pressing matter to discuss.

'I've got something for you. Its called *An Enquiry into the Obligations of Christians.* A bloke named William Carey has written it.'

Mill brushed away the information. 'This is old news!'

Bentham was surprised. 'Not to me,' he said.

Mill softened up and politely read the pamphlet that Bentham handed him. To break the uncomfortable silence, he read it aloud.

'For Whosoever shall call in the name of the Lord shall be saved. How then, shall they call on him, in whom they have not believed? How shall they believe in him, of whom they have not heard? And how shall they hear without a Preacher?'

Bentham shook his head! 'The Indians need reform, I can tell you that! I hear they burn women alive when the husband dies. Bloody pagans!'

'It's a lot worse than just that,' continued Mill. 'Their own rulers are divided; they cannot think beyond their small regions and would sell their neighbours if the need arose. They are myopic.'

'Haven't we announced that we are investing about 10,000 pounds in their education? Isn't that enough to civilize them?' asked Bentham imperiously.

'It is not that easy. They are a lot that does not allow progress to percolate down. They actively cultivate ignorance and superstition. "Progress" is a distant dream,' Mill summed up.

The men chatted for a bit. Mill's star was rising in the East India Company. He believed that theory precedes practice or "experience" and is not simply derived from it. In his massive three-volume *History of British India*, he asserted that his objectivity on the subject of India was guaranteed by the fact that he had never visited India![23] And yet, Mill is remembered as a potent force who drove policy in India in the nineteenth century.

Mill, through his writings, remained at the centre of power. He sat in the Company headquarters in London and 'managed to create an empire in writing'.

In the fifteen years that he spent at India House in Whitehall, London, Mill deeply influenced the administration and policies of the Empire, entirely through correspondence and dispatches.

So influential was Mill's utilitarianism and his writing that when Lord William Bentinck left London in 1828 to serve as the first governor-general of British India, he is said to have told Mill, 'I shall not be governor-general. It is you that will be.'

Mill's doctrine was quite simple: 'Hindoos were minstrels of perfidy and cowardice, and Muslims of sensuousness and promiscuity.'

The British treated the Indians exactly this way.

---

23 Arup Chatterjee, 'Lamb, Peacock and Mill: How a Bunch of Career Clerks Sitting in Company Headquarters in London, Who Never Visited India, Managed to Create an Empire in Writing', *The Hindu*, 23 March 2019

6

Shall We Educate the Indians?

The period between 1819 and 1830 is a significant one. It was during this period that James Mill rose to become the chief examiner of the East India Company in London and continued his efforts to 'civilize' India's population via his writing. He would exert a powerful influence on the ideology of the growing British Empire.

The governor-general of India at the time, Lord Hastings,[24] oversaw the fall of Peshwa Bajirao II and the end of the Maratha rule. This left the British in control of most of the Indian subcontinent. The Peshwa was exiled to Bithoor (Marat, near Kanpur, Uttar Pradesh) as a pensioner of the British. The Maratha heartland of Desh, including Pune, came under direct British rule.

---

24 Francis Rawdon-Hastings, first marquess of Hastings, served as the governor-general of India from 1813 to 1823.

Mountstuart Elphinstone[25] was in the thick of all this action. A benevolent man, he became the first governor of the Bombay Presidency[26] (1819–1827) and introduced measures to ensure peace between the erstwhile ruling classes of the Maratha confederacy and the general populace. Offered a large latitude by Lord Hastings, Elphinstone governed for nine long years as the commissioner of all Peshwa territories.

Now, Elphinstone had always been fundamentally clever; his cousin John Loch, who was a director in the East India Company, remembers: 'My impression of him, when we met on our respective holidays at the house of our uncle Adam, was that he was very quick and clever and could make himself master of any subject.'[27]

Elphinstone had grown to be a very astute administrator. He was painfully aware that the Peshwa, being a Brahmin himself, had inserted Brahmins into every aspect of administration with generous doles and by bequeathing lands. All of them hated the British. When he assumed office, one of his first acts as commissioner was to visit a temple. He then called an assembly

---

25 During the first thirty years of the nineteenth century the administrators gave British India the form it retained until 1947. Chief among them were Sir Thomas Munro in Madras, Mountstuart Elphinstone in western India, Sir Charles T. Metcalfe in Delhi and Holt Mackenzie, whose planning determined the lines of settlement from Benares to the Yamuna River. For keen students of history, Annexure 1 contains the 'Minute of Governor Sir Thomas Munro ordering the collection of detailed information on indigenous education'.

26 Geographically, the Bombay Presidency included both Bombay and Poona. One was the summer capital and other was the monsoon capital.

27 Sir Thomas Edward Colebrooke, *Memoir of the Honourable Mountstuart Elphinstone*, B. Quaritch, (Cornell University, 1861)

of the religious order and distributed presents to them to ensure that he would be able to function smoothly in the territory.

Soon, however, a conspiracy was unearthed. The Brahmins had joined hands with the military to bring Maratha power back to Poona. They murdered a group of Britishers in Poona and Satara. Elphinstone rounded up the perpetrators and ordered them to be punished in a brutal fashion—they were blown to their deaths from a cannon's mouth, an execution painless to them and horrific to onlookers.[28] Such a conspiracy against Elphinstone was never hatched again.

Over the next eighteen months, generous settlements were made to the military chiefs and jagirdars such that they would never find reason to revolt again. Elphinstone then appointed Captain H.D. Robertson as collector, magistrate and judge for the city of Poona. Several local people were appointed to responsible posts under the collector.

Once British authority was fully established, there was a constant demand from the collectors for daftardars[29] to carry out administrative work. So Elphinstone felt that the best thing would be to educate the natives for revenue work and offer them a salary of 1,000 rupees, a very high salary for a native but much less than what a Britisher would have to be paid.

Elphinstone knew that it would be difficult to get Englishmen for clerical jobs. Also, any locals that he employed in the

---

28 In *Scraps from my Sabretasche* (General Books, 2012), author George Carter Stent describes the 'most famous British punishment' as follows: '*The prisoner is generally tied to a gun with the upper part of the small of his back resting against the muzzle. When the gun is fired, his head is seen to go straight up into the air some forty or fifty feet; the arms fly off right and left, high up in the air, and fall at, perhaps, a hundred yards distance; the legs drop to the ground beneath the muzzle of the gun; and the body is literally blown away altogether, not a vestige being seen.*'

29 Revenue officers

administration could additionally serve as his ears on the ground. He was not inspired in the least by the thought that the locals 'could know to seek the Lord', as written in William Carey's essay, but only by the goal that they should provide cheap labour. The American Marathi Mission[30] had taken the lead in educating the masses in 1815 by opening the Hindoo Boys' school[31] with the help of some eminent Indians such as Framji Cowasji, Jagannath Shankarseth, Jamsetjee Jejeebhoy and others.

Elphinstone's initial thoughts on the education system in Poona were partly the result of the learnings from Bengal, the first province to fall to British rule. Bengal had proved the impossibility of establishing public schooling without substantial government support. Although many schools were set up thanks to subscriptions, donations and the work of missionaries and civil society to achieve maximum ends with minimal investments, once the initial enthusiasm waned, the schools that survived in Bengal were those that received government grants.

Elphinstone was hence pulled into a constant negotiation and renegotiation of what the colonial government's responsibility towards education was and what the states' role 'in the diffusion of education' was. Further, what was the role of missionaries and the 'spontaneous zeal of individuals'?

Hence, to make a beginning, in 1821, Elphinstone used a part of the Dakshina Fund, an official endowment for Brahmins

---

30 The American Marathi mission was set up in Bombay on 21 December 1813 by the American Board of Commissioners for Foreign Missions. Over time, it spread to hundreds of villages. The mission moved from Bombay to Ahmednagar in 1831. Cynthia Farrar, whom we will meet later, was a part of this.

31 Dr Arunchandra S. Pathak (ed.) *Greater Bombay District Gazetteer, 1986-1987, Vols 1,2 and 3,* (Government of Maharashtra).

during the Peshwa rule in western India,[32] to set up a Sanskrit college in Poona. The college was located in the residence of the last Peshwa ruler. This was an unprecedented use of the coveted Dakshina Fund. Sensing the beginning of a dangerous trend, a group of Chitpawan Brahmins[33] sought an appointment with Elphinstone. They were led by Limaye and Karandikar, local leaders who had come to plead their case.

Elphinstone was amused by the potbellied procession, but he was keen to know what they wished to discuss.

Limaye began in his usual self-important manner, 'Elphinstone Sahab, the Shashtras say clearly that a woman's brain is smaller than that of a man.'[34]

Karandikar added, 'Very true. Women shouldn't be given any kind of freedom as they are naturally fraudulent, liars, courageous, foolish and reckless. Their duty is to listen to the instructions of their husband and to serve him. If they are educated, it can lead to anartha.'[35]

Elphinstone found himself nodding. He knew well enough not to hurt the sensibilities of orthodox Indians (Brahmins continued to occupy positions of power in the administration). In any case, he didn't know why his visitors were discussing female education. There was no mandate from Britain to employ women as clerks in the government.

So he ventured to ask, 'Sirs, what specific concern has brought you here?'

---

32 Narender Kumar Sharma, 'Institution of Dakshina and its Impact on Sanskrit Education' in *Linguistic and Educational Aspirations under a Colonial System: A Study of Sanskrit Education during British Rule in India*, (Delhi: Concept Publishing House, 1976).

33 Chitpawan is a sub-caste of the Brahmin community.

34 This was also reported in newspapers in Poona at the time.

35 Marathi word for disaster.

Limaye jumped in, 'We have heard that you're planning to educate the masses. We want you to restrict this education to Brahmin men. The lower castes cannot do you any good. Like women, their brains are also small and underdeveloped.'

Karandikar added, 'Brahmins have always been part of the Maratha administration. We can help you run a tight ship.'

Elphinstone realized the immensity of the play they were making. He nodded pleasantly, spoke about the vision of his superiors in London to run an equitable state and sent them on their way. He knew, however, that the initiative to educate the masses would be met with much resistance because the social institutions and moral values were deeply rooted in the religious and casteist traditions of Poona. He also believed that any attempt to change them overnight would only create dissatisfaction among the people. Elphinstone was famously known for never acting in haste.

Nonetheless, he was in a bit of a rush that evening as he was to attend a dinner at the invitation of Lady Mary Falkland, the wife of a highly placed British official.

It was a typical soirée, where the conversations could be predicted in advance. Mosquitoes were usually part of the conversation.

'Aah, Commissioner. If only you could rid us of these infernal blister flies we have to tolerate in Poona,' she began as Elphinstone entered.

'Lady Falkland, my domain is sadly restricted to the command of men, not flies,' Elphinstone replied affably.

Lady Falkland wanted more news. 'What is it that I'm hearing of these jobs you're creating for the locals? Are they even going to have a bath before they come to work at your offices? It's bad enough to live here among them!'

'With the money we are paying them, they are sure to be able to afford soap of some kind.'

'But isn't giving them money and making them a part of the governing class something you must not do?' persisted Lady Falkland.

Elphinstone realized that the womenfolk must've been speculating much about this. 'I assure you, my Lady, that we have nothing to fear from the natives. They will be employed among the lowest rung of the clerical staff.'

Satisfied that she had enough information to share at the ladies' lunch the next day, Lady Falkland proceeded to ask her guests if any one of them could sing so she might persuade them to entertain the gathering. There was always an eager newcomer from England who would oblige.

At such parties, mosquito repellents were always a hot topic for discussion, as were experiences with ayahs and information gathered about the only person not in the room. Or the khus-khus mats[36] that made the afternoons bearable. In the presence of Elphinstone, topics of discussion included books, and the guests made sure that they knew enough about *Antigone*, a play by Sophocles that Elphinstone loved to talk about.

The missionaries present at such gatherings spoke about religious books too. In between laughs, one could hear the wives' conversations about the last letter sent back to England or complaining about the misfortune of staying back in Poona and what a hefty sacrifice it was indeed to do so![37] They spoke about

---

36 Khus-khus or vetiver mats or curtains helped to cool homes. Ayahs would sprinkle water on these curtains to keep a cool draught blowing into the home.

37 Nupur Chaudhuri, 'Memsahibs and their servants in nineteenth-century India', *Women's History Review*, Volume 3, Number 4, 1994.

what they had sewn and what they had painted and stifled their yawns with great effort. A guest from Bombay would inevitably declare that she had just watched *Miss in Her Teens*, *Padlock* and *The Road to Ruin*, absolutely delightful plays. This would make the Poona folks pity themselves even more as theatre hadn't arrived in Poona as yet.

As the party came to a close, palanquins gathered outside the home to haggle a price for taking guests home. The palanquin-bearers had a bad reputation for insubordination and their continual strikes for higher wages. If not promised fair compensation, they were liable to set the palanquin down in the middle of the journey and scamper off, leaving the passenger alone and fearing thieves, even though they were few in Poona.

The Brahmins were not always supporters of British rule, even though they were in its service. The British rulers knew this well.

'But nothing that we do now by way of education, emolument, or advancement in the public service at all satisfies the Chitpawans. They will never be satisfied till they regain their ascendancy in the country. But never have I known a national and political ambition, so continuous, so enduring, so far-reaching, so utterly impossible for us to satisfy, as that of the Brahmins of western India.'

—Sir Richard Temple, governor of Bombay, in his report of July 1879 to Lord Lytton, governor-general of India

Section 3

Khandoji Nevse Patil

In the nineteenth century, missionaries were allowed to set up schools in Bombay, Surat, Satara, Kolhapur and Ahmednagar far more freely than in Poona. The colonial capital of Poona was losing out to Bombay in many ways. For one, the opening of the trade route through Egypt made Bombay a key trading port. Second, the grip of the Brahmins was stronger in Poona.

Bombay, on the contrary, saw missionaries setting up vernacular free schools for boys. Even untouchables attended these schools. Similarly, the Dhera community in Surat and the Mahars in Ahmednagar had fewer prejudices against missionary schools. Around this time, many Mahars converted to Christianity.[38]

Poona remained relatively backward. Areas around Poona too were steeped in regressive social norms.

This section is set in 1831, in Naigaon, a prosperous village in Satara, Maharashtra. There was enough to go around in the village, and farmers, artisans and traders were able to earn a livelihood. As for its social structure, Naigaon was much closer to Poona rather than Bombay when it came to societal practices.

---

38 Rufus Andersen, *History of the Missions of the American Board of Commissioners for Foreign Missions to the Oriental Churches*, Volume II, (Fili Quarian Classics, 2010).

7
Naigaon

Khandoji Nevse was the village patil or head of Naigaon. The village Brahmins, especially the trio of Shastri, Gangal Kaka and Patwardhan, despised Khandoji and thought that he was a stooge of the British.

Gangal Kaka was a teacher in the Brahmin school in the village, and one never knew when he would relapse into reciting his own poetry. Potbellied Patwardhan was addicted to gluttony in a rather humorous way. He knew all the possible Sanskrit shlokas about the virtue of 'annadanam' or food donation, which he looked forward to the most.

'Annapurne sadapurne
Sankara-pranavallabhe
Gyanavairagya siddhyartham
Bhiksham dehi cha Parvati.'

(Annapurna Devi, Goddess of plentiful food
You are Lord Shiva's eternal Consort
Give us alms together with wisdom.)

Never once did he miss an opportunity to suggest that offering food to a Brahmin was the greatest deed one could do. As for Shastriji, he was a vile, vicious, wizened vazir. He was a chess master who would think five moves ahead of anyone and believed that it was his misfortune that he was saddled with two complete idiots like Gangal and Patwardhan.

As it happened, Khandoji's wife Lakshmi was due to deliver any day. While Lakshmi and Khandoji's mother Aaisaheb prayed for a son, it was clear that Khandoji wanted a daughter. It was this pleasant thought that was going through Khandoji's mind as he was tying his red pagdi, when Mahar[39] Sonkamble came running into his house.

'Khandoji, you must come with me. Tambe is going to the well to drown his newborn daughter,' Sonkamble blurted.

Khandoji's mother, Aaisaheb, heard this and came out of her room.

---

39 The Mahars are considered to be the original inhabitants of Maharashtra. They performed functions such as watchmen, trackers of thieves, street sweepers, messengers, wall menders, adjudicators of boundary disputes and suppliers of coarse cloth to the village. In return for these services, the village granted them a watan, or rights to a small piece of land to do their own cultivation. The watan also included a share of village produce. They also worked at times as agricultural labourers. The Mahars were traditionally a fearless people. It was Shivaji Maharaj who first recognized them for their loyalty and bravery and recruited several of them into his army in the seventeenth century. Later, during the colonial period, large numbers of Mahars and Dhors were recruited for military duties by the East India Company and the British Raj.

'Then let him drown his daughter in the well. Why do all of you come running here at the slightest provocation? It is Tambe's daughter. He will do as he deems fit,' she said unfeelingly.

Khandoji ignored his mother's comment and hurriedly finished tying his pagdi, calling out, 'Sonkamble, wait for me.'

Aaisaheb slapped her forehead with her palm and sighed in resigned despair. Ever since some Gora Sahab had appointed him the patil, Khandoji appeared to have unlocked some latent reserves of responsibility.

Meanwhile, Khandoji and Sonkamble reached the well just in time.

Khandoji was breathless but spoke with urgency, 'Arre Tambe, what are you doing!'

Tambe was in tears. 'Patil Sahab, please don't stop me. Let me give this girl mukti, let me free her from her fate. I have no food in my house.'

Tambe's wife Gajri was deeply distressed as she tried to wrest her daughter from her husband.

'Then I will help you find a job. What mukti will you get by drowning your daughter? Have you forgotten that it was a woman who gave birth to you? If we start drowning all our newborn daughters in wells, then even sons won't be born. It will be the end of this world,' said Khandoji, trembling with indignation.

'I am not talking about the whole world. In my small world, I have nothing to feed her, no dowry to get her married and neither can this girl support me in my old age. I cannot bear this burden. You will understand me only if you have a daughter of your own, Khandoji,' said Tambe with indignation.

'Arre Tambe, your Lakshmi vahini is expecting. I'm hoping that Khandoba blesses my house with a daughter. Everything in this world that is kind and beautiful and selfless is because of women. Imagine if the world only had people like you and I. We would have found so many reasons to kill each other and not care,' implored Khandoji.

Khandoji's words seemed to strike a chord with Tambe, and he started thinking about what Khandoji had said. Using this moment of distraction, Tambe's wife Gajri finally snatched their daughter from his hands and ran back to their home. Realizing that he would not be able to muster the courage to come back again and drown his newborn, Tambe's shoulders drooped.

He spoke with a lump in his throat, 'Khandoji, what you did today is wrong. You may be the patil of this village, but now I am stuck with a curse for the rest of my life! And I hope a daughter is born to you too so you understand how I feel!'

Khandoji knew that there was nothing he could say at that moment to make things better. But he hoped that Tambe would come to his senses.

Instead of going home, Tambe went to work. He was employed by a zamindar to keep unwanted stray animals at bay and keep his farm and his lands safe. Tambe was a sincere and punctual person. That day, a part of the zamindar's boundary wall had been damaged, and Tambe wanted to fix it before animals entered to plunder the fields. But his mind was simply not up to that task. He felt weighed down. So he stopped working on the wall and started walking aimlessly along it, cursing his destiny. Eventually, he picked up a rock and started throwing it at an imaginary target.

It was as he was doing this that Shastriji and Patwardhan saw him from afar. They had heard about Tambe setting out to drown his daughter and Khandoji stopping it. They called out to him.

'Arre, achut Tambe,' Patwardhan yelled. 'What are you doing so far out on the road? Can't you see Shastriji is coming? If your shadow falls on Shastriji, he will have to return home and have a bath!'

Tambe's thoughts were elsewhere, but he quickly bowed his head and retreated to the wall.

Shastriji chimed in, 'It is clear that you're neglecting your work. This kind zamindar has given work to an untouchable like you, and you have no respect for it. I curse you, you will be born as a fly in your next birth.'

Tambe was petrified. 'I'm so sorry, Brahmin Devata. Please don't make me a fly in my next birth!'

Shastriji shook his head with mock finality. 'Now nothing can be done about it!'

Tambe pleaded, 'Isn't there anything I can do that will save me from a Brahmin Devata's curse?'

After a pretence at deep thought, Shastriji signalled to Patwardhan who spoke with great condescension, 'You can catch a snake and bring it to us by evening.'

'But how will I catch a snake?' Tambe cried.

Patwardhan was indignant. 'You asked me for a way out and I gave it. Now it's up to you. If you don't listen to me, then your wife and that infernal daughter of yours will also be born as flies in their next birth, and all of you will be eaten by the same snake!'

Tambe clutched his head in despair. Could this day get any worse?

Tambe knew he had no recourse. 'Where should I bring it?' he asked.

Patwardhan nodded. 'You catch it, put it in a basket and come to Shastriji's house. Then I will tell you what to do. But this must be done today!'

Tambe was seen walking towards the forest. But no one saw him coming out.

8

Only a Son Can Take You Vaitarni Paar

Aaisaheb was praying. 'O Khandoba, my Khando is a silly boy. Don't listen to him. If he has a daughter, who will take him Vaitarni paar?[40]

Khandoji saw his mother in prayer but was in no mood to argue with her objections to his desire for a daughter. It wasn't really in his hands whether a son or a daughter was born to them. Besides, matters of the village needed attending too; several people had come to meet him. Gavli Mang[41] had also come and was waiting to talk to him about an abhanga[42] written by the Varkari Sant Tukaram.

40 It is believed that to attain swarga or heaven, one has to cross the Vaitarni River and that only a son can help his father do this.

41 The Mang was a caste of rope-makers and village entertainers. They worshipped Goddess Bhavani and for their services they received a share of the village produce.

42 Devotional poetry

'Sing for us my friend, so we may learn something,' Khandoji said.

Gavli closed his eyes and sang with passion.

'Avgha toh shakun, Hrudayi Devache Chintan
Yethe nasto viyoga, Labha Une Kaay Mag?
Chhand Harichya namacha, shuchirboot sada vacha
Tuka mhane Harichya dasa, shubhkaal avghya disha.'
(Every moment that you take God's name
You feel a oneness with the divine.
Whatever the task, when the chant of God is constant.
Tuka says to the disciple, God's actions flow through you.)

When he opened his eyes, everyone was clapping except Aaisaheb. Gavli's appeal to keep God in one's heart and embrace one's good fortune fell on deaf ears!

Aisaheb said, 'Gavli, if you believe in God, explain to my Khandoji what a disaster he is wishing for. A daughter!'

Gavli laughed. 'I just sang about keeping Vitthala in our hearts and speaking auspicious words, Aaisaheb. What can I add to what Tukaram says?'

Aaisaheb was exasperated. 'Is there no one who can put some sense into my son?'

As if on cue, Patwardhan cleared his throat. He was standing at the main gate. Everyone stood up. Aaisaheb retreated inside.

Patwardhan's voice boomed, 'I have just come to say that there will be a Sati Ma amongst us soon! We should all prepare to worship her and take her to the fire.'

Khandoji was confused about this great prediction. Patwardhan was a slimy character. But he was just a mouthpiece. It was the wily mind of Shastriji that was lightning quick. He always had an argument to justify his propaganda of fear.

Gavli asked, 'Did someone die?'

Patwardhan dismissed the question with a flick of his wrist.

'Gavli, don't forget you're a Mang. You don't have the right to question a Brahmin. Do you even know how your greedy community got its name? When Sant Jambrishi set one of you to guard his cow, your man ate the cow instead of watching her! Greedy Mangs! Misfortune is all you can bring!'

'Brahmin Devata,' Khandoji interjected, 'we were all merely enjoying an evening of Sant Tukaram's abhangas. Is there something you want to tell us?'

'I already told you! There is a woman who will be blessed as Sati Mata soon. This is Shastriji's jyotishwani, his prediction. God's will. Shambho Shambho!' So saying, Patwardhan left.

Unknown to Khandoji, Aaisaheb later went to meet Shastriji and asked him for a solution to her own predicament. She wanted a grandson, but Khandoji was praying for a girl. Shastriji pretended to be in deep meditation to arrive at a solution, then whispered his view into Patwardhan's ears.

As instructed by Shastriji, Patwardhan guided Aaisaheb to offer annadanam and dakshina to three Brahmins so Khandoji would beget a son.

'Annadanam samam danam
Trilokeshu na vidhathe.'
(Annadanam is supreme and incomparable to any charity.)

A harried Aaisaheb went home to arrange a lavish meal for the Brahmins. There were very few households in the village that had the wherewithal to offer puri, bhaaji, halwa, kheer and laddoo, and Khandoji's house was one of those. A good meal would be served.

And Shastriji's plan to revive Sati was underway as well.

9

Shastriji Lays a Trap

Shatriji's master plan was to revive Sati in the village and instil fear.

'Patwardhan, let us organize a sabha where we will teach four important precepts: first, as we Brahmins have outlived the Peshwas, we are clearly smarter. Second, we know how to use the shastras for our own benefit. Third, the British had no business abolishing Sati. They don't understand our traditions! And finally, a woman without a husband is a walking temptation for any man who desires her. It is better that she dies. Hence, Sati is highly beneficial.'

Patwardhan was nodding and taking notes.

'We must gather everyone for this sabha,' Shastriji continued. 'Because of these British and their puppets like Khandoji, the grip of dharma is loosening. If this continues, the Brahmins will soon meet the same fate as the Peshwas—irrelevance. I cannot let that happen,' he thundered.

Meanwhile, Gajri was getting anxious as the night advanced. Where was Tambe? She gathered a couple of neighbours and walked to where Tambe worked. To her chagrin, she met the zamindar, his irate employer.

'Your husband did not do a thing today! He was floating around aimlessly. I saw Patwardhan and Shastriji scolding him for neglecting his duties. Served him right, so I did not want to intervene. Go and ask them what happened!'

There was no way Gajri and her Mahar friends could go to the Brahmin locality. The Brahmins would set the dogs on them if they could! She spent an anxious night waiting for her husband. She couldn't wait to show him that their daughter was soft as cotton, her face clear as the full moon and her smile as radiant as a garden full of flowers. And since their daughter had liberated them from their loneliness and herself from a disastrous fate, she wished to name her 'Mukta'. Now if only Tambe would return! She sat by her doorstep to wait for him and eventually fell asleep there.

The next day, Khandoji heard about Gajri's predicament and learnt from an evasive Patwardhan that he had seen Tambe go towards the forest. Khandoji immediately sent a search party, fearing the worst.

By late evening, Tambe's body was recovered. He had died of snakebite. Why would Tambe go into the forest in the first place? Khandoji decided to confront Shastriji. He visited him.

'Brahmin Devata, we found out that Tambe entered the forest after being scolded by you. Do you know why?'

Shastriji burped. 'Good question. You want me to explain the behaviour of all the stupid people in the world?'

Khandoji was persistent. 'My apologies, Brahmin Devata. Maybe I said it wrong. Was there any conversation between you and Tambe that might have resulted in him going to the forest?'

Shastriji screamed, 'Tambe was an idiot. How would I know why he went to the forest? But now, you answer my question. Why are you asking me about this insignificant Mahar and spoiling the purity of my mouth? Shambho, Shiva Shambho.'

Shastriji grabbed a glass of water, gargled loudly and spat out the water forcefully.

Khandoji carried on, 'We found Tambe in the forest. He died of snakebite.'

Shastriji pretended to pray, 'Shambho, Shiva Shambho!'

Khandoji remarked, 'Yes, it is very unfortunate.'

'Unfortunate?' Shastriji barked. 'Can't you see? It is you who are a murderer. Destiny had ordained that one member of that family must die. You saved the daughter, so Naag Devata took matters into his own hands and killed the father. None of you have any knowledge of the shastras and dharma. Your obsequiousness to the British is disgusting! You're just a Patil, I'm a Brahmin—a representative of the gods. I can see what the gods are thinking and what they're doing. They speak through me.'

'My knowledge of the shastras cannot equal yours. But I do know that I saved a life, not ended one. There's a piece of the puzzle missing here.'

Shastriji turned away decisively, indicating that the conversation had come to its conclusion. For him at least.

10

Gajri Takes a Decision

The mood at Tambe's house was sombre. Gajri was sobbing uncontrollably with Mukta on her lap, and the neighbours were gathered all around. Seemingly from nowhere, Gokhale appeared at the scene. He was a junior priest training under Shastriji.

He looked straight at Gajri. 'Shastriji had foreseen that you will be magically transformed from an untouchable to a goddess. You are now Goddess Sati, the saviour of all,' he said with fake reverence and folded hands as he rang a brass puja bell incessantly.

Then he addressed the crowd, 'You fools, you are in the presence of a goddess. Don't you know that you must bow to her?'

The clueless crowd did as he bid. Gajri was confused. Was this man trying to burn her alive in the process of making her a goddess? She could sense the expectation that she had to accept her fate.

As the villagers prepared for Tambe's last rites, Gajri realized that her hands were being tied by Gokhale's stooges. She was standing a few feet away from the pyre. In the absence of a son, Tambe's pyre was to be lit by one of his community. To everyone's surprise, Shastriji arrived at the scene and stood at some distance, as did Khandoji who had made the arrangements for the last rites.

Shastriji proclaimed, 'Sati Maiyya ki jai ho (Hail Sati Maiyya)!'

Khandoji intervened, 'Brahmin Devata, has Gajri agreed to become Sati?'

Shastriji brushed his question aside. 'I'm tired of your objections to dharma, Khandoji. You may be a Patil but you are ignorant. Are you saying you know more than I do?'

Khandoji's posture became defiant. 'Not about the shastras, but about the law, yes. Two years ago, Sati was abolished under the law.'

Shastriji mocked him, 'Fine. Then go and bring your gora officer here to stop this. Until then, let me explain to Gajri what it means to become Sati Maiyya.'

He turned to Gajri. 'You will have seven births, and if you become Sati today, in all the seven births that you take hereafter, you will be suhagan. You will never become a widow again. Sati is your birthright!'

Khandoji was now livid. 'Shastriji, look around. You are two Brahmins here today and we are twenty villagers. You know the shastras and we know the law. So let Gajri decide whether she wants to become Sati or not. But you must promise me that if she says no, you will never again ask a woman from this village to burn herself alive on her husband's pyre.'

Khandoji turned to the men.

'Can any of you even imagine the sacrifice we ask of our women? Can you imagine what would happen if you were burnt alive? Shastriji, forget about us. You are Brahmin Devata. Can you imagine what would happen if someone set fire to your dhoti?'

Shastriji was furious at the suggestion.

'Khandoji, you are not only ignorant, but you are insulting me and depriving this poor woman of a bhavya mrityu, a glorious, pious death, and reincarnation as a suhaagan. Gajri, in your decision lies the future of this village. If you don't become a Sati today, I curse you with vaidhavya, widowhood, for your next seven births.'

Gokhale added, 'Gajri, you will bring all the horrors of fate upon yourself if you do not become Sati today. Sit on your husband's pyre and I will light it. This is a religious ceremony, and we will perform it with the most sacred of mantras. Did you ever imagine that your death would be so glorious?'

The musicians called by Shastriji started playing the drums. The atmosphere was charged and Gajri started to feel the heat of the situation.

Finally, she said, 'Brahmin Devata, I have no knowledge. I am ignorant. So forgive me. But who will take care of Mukta? You can curse me for the next seven births, but if I become Sati today, I will curse my own daughter to live as an orphan.'

Sonkamble, who had been standing behind Khandoji all this while, rushed forward to untie Gajri's hands.

'They say that women and Sudras belong to low caste. But when you say that God dwells everywhere, then is he not in the heart of the Sudra? Has not a Sudra come from the same place as the Brahmin? Is he not also composed of five elements? Has he no birth, has he no death? You are misguided when you say that a Sudra belongs to the lowest class.'[43]

—Sant Eknath, Hindu saint, philosopher and poet. He was a devotee of Lord Vitthala and is a major figure of the Warkari tradition of Maharashtra

43 Hulas Singh, *Rise of Reason: Intellectual History of 19th-century Maharashtra*, (Taylor & Francis, 2015).

Section 4

A Revolution Takes Birth

Khandoji's wish to have a daughter was to be fulfilled soon. She was going to be a livewire named Savitri.

Observe how different her mindset is, right from her childhood. Note the significance of Saguna Kshirsagar, who becomes a major inspiration behind the work of Savitri and her future mentor.

11

Khandoji's Mulgi

Naigaon, near Poona, 1837

Gajri had nowhere to go. So Khandoji took her and Mukta home. He imagined that with Lakshmi pregnant, Gajri would help around the house. Besides, it wasn't unusual for village patils to have servants in those days.

As they entered the house, Khandoji was apprehensive about the fact that Gajri was an untouchable.[44] But the scene that met him at home was one of intense suspense. Lakshmi was in labour and Aaisaheb was alone at home. She was so relieved to

44 Gajri was a Mahar. The Mahars were assigned the work of removing dead cows from the village. The community started eating the flesh of cows that had died naturally, and the eating of beef formed the basis for the caste being treated as untouchables.

see another woman, any woman, that she immediately took her inside to help with Lakshmi's labour and delivery.

Khandoji was left holding little Mukta. He started pacing the room, hoping that Sonkamble or his wife would miraculously appear so he could hand over the child. Lakshmi's screams were getting louder and louder, until the last one, which wasn't Lakshmi's scream.

Aaisaheb emerged slowly from Lakshmi's room, fearful and forlorn. She gave Khandoji an empty stare, the pallu of her sari covering her mouth and said, '*Mulgi hui hai.*'

Khandoji's reaction was a study in contrast to hers. He shouted with glee and said, 'Sonkamble, go bring laddoos. Lakshmi Mata has come into my house. We must organize a janmotsav to celebrate the birth of my daughter.'

Aaisaheb almost fainted at the idea. A janmotsav? For a mulgi, a daughter? She quietly left to meet Shastriji to ask him how to prevent this ridiculous janmotsav that Khandoji was planning.

Aaisaheb spoke between tears, 'Shastriji, some evil eye of unimaginable proportions has befallen us. Even after your guidance, a mulgi has been born to Khandoji.'

Shastriji feigned concern, 'Aaisaheb, I don't know how to tell you this. Your son did not allow Gajri's offering to Sati Mata. What did you expect? Khandoji has gone against dharma in every way. It is only because you performed annadanam that Lakshmi, your daughter-in-law, is alive and well. Khandoji does not understand how your intervention and our prayers saved him.'

Aaisaheb was trembling with rage. 'Gajri? I will remove her from my house, Brahmin Devata.'

Shastriji nodded and pretended to seek divine input. He was secretly happy that a girl had been born to Khandoji, as this would allow him to continue his reign of fear over Aaisaheb.

Patwardhan whispered into Shastriji's ear. Was there any chance that they could get another meal out of Aaisaheb? Shastriji glared at him and said to Aaisaheb, 'I can see that Gajri is a walking-talking apshagun, a bad omen, in your house.'

Aaisaheb howled, 'Arre Deva, why did I let her help me with the delivery? There was no one else at home at the time.'

Shastriji did not know this. But it fell nicely into his narrative. He drew in his breath sharply as if to show immense consternation.

'An untouchable was involved in the birth of your grandchild! As your Brahmin Devata, I can see into the future. If you remove Gajri from your house, Lakshmi will give you a grandson soon.'

Aaisaheb nodded and left. Gokhale was secretly happy. He had had an eye on Gajri for a while now. As long as she was under Khandoji's protection, he could not do anything.

When she returned home, Aaisaheb raised a ruckus.

She told Khandoji with finality, 'I don't want to hear any arguments. You have to remove Gajri and Mukta's evil influence from our house. Also, if you organize a janmotsav, I will not participate. It is unheard of to celebrate a daughter's birth in this way. You have lost your mind!'

Khandoji was expecting this, and he had already made arrangements to have the abandoned house just behind his own home fixed up so Gajri and Mukta could live there. Their old house belonged to the zamindar, and he had decided to rent it to someone else.

Then, to announce his happiness at being blessed with a daughter, Khandoji decided to address the people of the village.

'Today, I have been blessed with a mulgi, and I want to name her Savitri. It was Savitri who brought her husband Satyavan back to life, freeing him from the clutches of the Lord of Death, Yama Raj. My Savitri will be a suhagan all her life.'

There was appreciation for the sentiment and clapping all around.

'I have another request from all of you. Gajri is our sister and Mukta is our daughter. All of us have to support her and Mukta by giving them shelter and work so they can live a life of dignity. And together, let us resolve that when Mukta becomes ten years old, we will all find a proper husband for her and get her married.'

As per Khandoji's instructions, the people of the village planted several fruit trees and a vegetable garden around Gajri's new house. It was Gajri's job to tend to them.

Khandoji himself planted a sapling.

He told Sonkamble, 'I have performed the janmostav of Savitri by planting this sapling and offering shelter to another daughter. Perhaps helping each other has greater value than performing rituals.'

Thus, he marked Savitri's birth.

12

Savitri Learns on the Side

As Savitri and Mukta grew older, they found company in each other. They played together. There were many games that kept them busy; one was played with sticks and small pebbles, another was a variation of hopscotch, and there were all kinds of role-playing games in which Savitri was always dispensing justice. They spent all their free time together. However, Savitri had a very curious mind. One day, she took Mukta and snuck out of their home to visit the Brahmin pathshala, the school for Brahmins only, where Gangal Kaka taught. A group of six boys with chalks and slates sat before him. Savitri would hide and listen to the lesson. After a couple of days, Mukta told her that she could not accompany her any more as if she were caught, she and her mother might be asked to leave the village. Savitri tried to reason with her but Mukta was too scared to listen.

One morning, at the pathshala, Gangal Kaka was instructing the class.

'Yesterday, we learnt "प". Today, we will learn "पे".' He started writing on the blackboard.

The boys were bored out of their skins, but they copied what he wrote nevertheless.

'Repeat after me, "*Vidya dadanti vinayam, vinyad yati patratam.* (Knowledge gives discipline, from discipline comes worthiness.)"'

The boys repeated after Gangal Kaka.

When the lesson for the day concluded, one of the boys, Kelkar, checked to see if the girl who hid behind the tree and copied everything was still there. He and one of his friends waited for Gangal Kaka to leave. Then they went up to her, threatening, 'Ae, mulgi. You know you're not supposed to be here.'

'Why?' Savitri demanded.

Pointing at her, Kelkar said, 'I've seen you here all of last week. If you were allowed to be here in the first place, wouldn't you be sitting in the classroom with us? Yet, you're hiding behind the tree and copying everything!'

Savitri was not one to be put down easily. 'So what? I know as much as you do.'

Kelkar felt insulted. 'I'll tell Gangal Kaka that you think you know as much as we do. Let's see what he does.'

Savitri knew that would be the end of her learning. So she thought quickly and asked, 'What do you want? If you wanted to complain, you would've already complained.'

Kelkar had a sweet tooth. So he said, 'If you get me something sweet to eat every day, I won't complain to Gangal Kaka.'

'You want a sweet every day? Havrat—greedy boy! Don't you get food at home?'

Kelkar shook his head and started to walk away. 'It's useless talking to you. If you come here tomorrow and there's no sweet for me, I will expose you, and Gangal Kaka will beat you up.'

Savitri stood with her arms akimbo. 'Ae, nobody beats me up. My father is the patil of this village.'

Shubham chuckled. 'Oh good, now I know who you are. Easier for me to complain. Bye!'

Kelkar and his buddy walked away as Savitri stuck her tongue out at them in disgust.

Even though she was worried that Kelkar might tell Gangal Kaka about her, she continued to revise and recite the alphabet. But her mind was racing. She had always been the apple of her father's eye. If only he would allow her to study! And what sweet could she take for that fat Kelkar tomorrow?

When she returned home, her father had gone out for the day, so she couldn't pester him to buy her something sweet. He never said no to her. But now she had to come up with something else. She thought of trying a new trick. Mother was busy with her tailoring. So all she had was her grandmother.

Savitri's face was serious as she said, 'Aaji, I've realized that I should learn cooking!'

Aaji looked at Savitri, stupefied. 'Vitthala, I never thought this day would come. Take me away.'

Savitri pressed on, 'I mean it, Aaji. You know I like to learn new things.'

Aaji was not convinced. 'I know that. But you are always drawing something in that book of yours.'

Savitri put her arms around her grandmother and said with wide-eyed innocence, 'Yes. But I want to learn everything about the swayampak ghar (kitchen).'

Aaji relented. 'Come, I will teach you how to make poli today.'

This wasn't going according to plan. Savitri said, 'No, no, not poli. I want to learn how to make laddoos.'

'Aah! Now comes the real reason. Out with it! Why do you want to make laddoos?' Aaji demanded.

'Because Baba always says I will get married into a rich house. I won't have to make polis. I will only have to cook on special occasions,' said Savitri sweetly.

Aaji laughed out loud. There was such innocence to Savitri's beliefs that she didn't want to break her fantasy bubble. She walked away, murmuring that laddoos were indeed made for special occasions, so there was no reason to make them today.

Aaji went for her afternoon siesta, which left Savitri wondering where she would get her laddoos from. Her prayers were answered in the evening. Her father returned with a gift for her—a new drawing book and a box of sweets.

However, the next day when she visited the school with a laddoo to bribe the greedy Kelkar, Gangal Kaka caught her.

He grabbed her by the shoulder and screamed, 'Savitri, if I ever see you here again, the consequences will be dire. It will be the death of your father and your future husband.'

Savitri was heartbroken! Her father meant the world to her. Sobbing helplessly, she swore never to go to Gangal Kaka's school again.

13

Officer Lizzit Visits Naigaon

Lizzit was a senior officer in the British civil service and worked in the education department. He was a kind soul. He was passionate about educating the locals. Not only was this part of his job, but he was also personally interested in spreading education and ran his own library in Poona.

As part of his work, he visited Naigaon and was keen to send a team of missionaries there to open schools in the area. He wanted to meet the patil of the village. So, Khandoji went to meet him.

Lizzit welcomed Khadoji and said, 'You're doing very good work in your village by implementing the Abolition of Sati Act.'

'Thank you, Lizzit Sahab.'

'But keeping women alive isn't enough. You have to help us educate them. I had sent Sister Margaret to your village to help you open a school,' said Lizzit.

Khandoji remembered vividly how Shastriji, Gangal Kaka and Patwardhan had all but driven Sister Margaret out of the village.

Lizzit continued, 'What I will never forget is that Sister Margaret told us that your daughter is the most courageous person in the village and has a strong desire to learn. So why did you not enrol her in the school?'

Khandoji nodded and said, 'I'm sorry, Lizzit Sahab. The village Brahmins told my mother that I would die if my daughter Savitri got an education. So she did not let me enrol Savitri in Sister Margaret's school. Later, Savitri told me that Gangal Kaka, the teacher, told her the same thing.'

Tea and some cookies were served.

After they had each taken a cup, Khandoji continued, 'I gave Sister Margaret a place to run the school, and I also called the Panchayat Sabha and pleaded that children of all jaatis[45] should be allowed to attend school. But being the patil is not enough. The Brahmins are much more powerful when it comes to the social aspects of village life.'

Lizzit sipped his tea and asked, 'Do you think you will die if your daughter gets an education?'

Khandoji was a humble man. 'I don't know what is written in the shastras. It is confusing, no doubt. Sister Margaret is educated, and she said that her father is very much alive. She has also travelled so far from her home, so she must be very passionate about education. I have heard that other American and English women are also here to spread education. Maybe the shastras are specific to us?'

---

45 Jaati is another word for caste.

Lizzit implored, 'But you can set an example by educating your daughter. She's just eight years old. And this death of the father is utter nonsense!'

'Our dharma doesn't allow it, Lizzit Sahab. When Sister Margaret visited, Shastriji himself came to the sabha and told us that there would be famine in the village if we educated the girls and there would be an epidemic of haiza, cholera, if we allowed Shudras to attend school along with the Brahmins. I have no knowledge of how true these things are. But being the patil of the village, how can I take the risk?'

Officer Lizzit understood what was happening. As long as the Brahmins could predict dire consequences by twisting the shashtras any way they wanted, they could get people to obey them. He persisted patiently.

'Let me explain this another way. How did you know I wished to meet you?'

Khandoji thought for a moment and said, 'From your letter.'

'But did you read it yourself?'

'No. I went to Gangal Kaka who read it to me. Brahmins never lie.'

Lizzit couldn't believe his ears. 'Is that so? Who told you that?'

Khandoji said earnestly, 'Brahmin Devata are our connection to God. How can we doubt what they say?'

Lizzit knew he was close to making Khandoji see reason. He asked, 'So, did this man who read my letter out to you not tell you that I had asked you to bring your daughter along?'

Khandoji's face fell. He had had no idea.

Lizzit smiled as he drove his point home, 'Gangal did not tell you the whole truth about the letter. Likewise, isn't it possible that he's not telling you the entire truth about the shastras? The reason I asked you to come here with your daughter is that Sister Margaret wanted her to have a copy of the Bible.'

Khandoji's eyes were full of tears. He broke down at the mere thought of keeping Savitri from anything.

Lizzit continued after a brief pause, 'All I'm saying is that it should be evident to you that your Brahmins have their cake and eat it too. None of you can read and verify what they're saying. Obviously, if any of you began to read, their power would end. That's the "famine" and "cholera" for the Brahmins—not for the village. All over the world, children are attending schools without even knowing what caste they belong to. Is there famine because of that? The two are completely unconnected.'

Khandoji was absorbing Lizzit's words. Finally, he said, 'I cannot deny that you are making sense. Maybe I should have brought Savitri along to meet you. She is the only one who can ask more questions than you.'

The two men laughed.

Khandoji continued, 'I cannot cross the line of dharma. But I will be more aware and open to change, even though it will be a hard-fought battle.'

Lizzit understood that Khandoji was going out on a limb even in making such a simple promise.

Lizzit ploughed on, 'Learning to write is just another type of drawing. Do you prevent your daughter from making shapes with sticks in the soil?'

Khandoji understood. The two men finished their tea and parted ways, each uncomfortable that they had not been able to convince the other entirely of their point of view and yet happy that they did not fully disagree either.

Lizzit returned to Poona the next day and thought about sharing this conversation with his friend James Mitchell.

14

Saguna Kshirsagar

Missionary James Mitchell[46] and his wife, Margaret Mitchell, had invited Officer Lizzit for lunch. Margaret Mitchell had recently begun to superintend the Scottish Mission's girls' schools in Poona.[47]

A local widow, Saguna Kshirsagar, would often help Margaret Mitchell with odd jobs around the house. Saguna's cousin

---

46 There is often confusion between John Murray Mitchell and James Mitchell. James was a colleague of Reverend Dr John Murray Mitchell, often referred to as Murray Mitchell, another Scottish missionary and Orientalist who was sent to Bombay, India, to join some missionary colleagues of the Church of Scotland in November 1838. Murray Mitchell set up a Scottish Mission in Nagpur and soon mastered Marathi. He also studied Sanskrit. John married Maria Mitchell in 1842. Maria Murray Mitchell wrote many books such as *Bala Soonderee Tagore: A Narrative of the Conversion of a Hindoo lady to the Christian Religion* and *In Southern India: A Visit to Some of the Chief Mission Stations in the Madras Presidency.* They returned to Scotland in 1846 and returned to India between 1849 and 1856.

47 Jana Tschurenev, *Empire, Civil Society and the Beginnings of Colonial Education in India,* (Cambridge University Press, 2019).

Govindrao was Jyotirao Phule's father. Saguna was an adoptive mother to Jyotirao.

Margaret was very fond of Saguna, who worked hard and always had a smile on her face.

Saguna and Margaret were preparing for Officer Lizzit's arrival. Saguna had made some kokum sherbet to serve to the guests.

This had become something of a tradition—several diaries kept by memsahibs in British times credit the local folk in Poona for introducing sherbets to the British. There was chincheche sarbat (tamarind sherbet), limbache sarbat (lemon sherbet), valyache sarbat (khus sherbet) and kairiche panhe (raw mango sherbet). Mrs Mitchell gladly welcomed these additions to their luncheons as they took care of the need for a welcome drink when guests would settle and converse before lunch.

For the lunch with Officer Lizzit, the cook had prepared a simple meal. First, a serving of craigie toast and cold soup. Then a serving of roast chicken and finally a caramel custard that looked pleasantly firm, unlike one of regrettable appearance that cooks were quick to dish out if they felt the memsahib wasn't looking. The Mitchells were preparing for a pleasant afternoon of catching up.

As they settled down to conversation, Lizzit asked, 'How are things at the school?'

Margaret's favourite topic! 'My school is but a drop in the ocean. We simply do not have enough schools to take care of the large population here.'

James chimed in, 'India is teeming with people, Lizzit. What's your guess on the numbers here?'

Lizzit was well informed. 'I recently read that Poona had just 25,000 residents in 1700. By 1800, the population had grown to 1,00,000. That's equal to Copenhagen, bigger than New York and a little smaller than Marseilles; but either way, a large place.'[48]

---

48 Manu Pillai, 'Opinion: The Peshwas and Their Capital', LiveMint, 23 February 2019.

James whistled. 'A population that just does not understand what's good for it.'

'True. I had sent Sister Margaret to a village called Naigaon to start a school. Only one girl showed up and that too, not to enrol, but to ask questions. She had been told her father would die if she enrolled. The patil of the village is helpless against the threats of famine and infectious epidemics that would befall them if girls and the lower castes went to school. It's appalling, really!'

'I'm surprised that a girl even showed up! Such spunk,' said James.

'Would you believe it! It was the same patil's daughter, no less,' Lizzit finished his story.

Margaret was excited on hearing about Savitri. 'We must bring this girl here and admit her to the Scottish Mission School. I can enrol so many more girls, if only their parents would come forward.'

Saguna overheard all of this. All she could think about was that there could be no better match for her Jyoti than this girl who had such a great desire to learn.

The trio had a pleasant lunch discussing the new books that had arrived in Lizzit's personal library—Thomas Paine's *The Rights of Man* and Plato's *The Republic* and *The Apology of Socrates.*

After lunch, Lizzit opened up copies of the new books he had received for the Scottish Mission School library and a paper with a fresh poem by William Wordsworth.

He read the poem out loud.

'Fair scenes, erewhile, I taught a happy child,
The echoes of your rocks, my carols wild:
The spirit sought not then, in cherished sadness,
A cloudy substitute for failing gladness,

In youth's keen eye the livelong day was bright,
The sun at morning, and the stars at night,
Alike, when first the bittern's hollow bill
Was heard, or woodcocks roamed the moonlight hill.'

Margaret mused, '"I taught a happy child"—isn't that the best line.'

Lizzit chipped in, 'The one about the youth's keen eye making the livelong day bright is beautiful too.'

Margaret conceded, 'Wordsworth does have a way with words. Officer Lizzit, I've been reading a bit of Indian history and apparently, Maratha women haven't always been treated this way. Their stories have been full of fortitude. Jijamata was a very wise mother to the famed Maratha ruler Shivaji. Ahilyabai Holkar shaped Indore. And Maharani Durgavati fought against Akbar's vast army. The people we meet every day, like her,' she indicated Saguna, who was clearing the table, 'would be inspired if they learnt that women have always been revered in these lands.'

Saguna was listening to everything. In her simple white cotton saree with a white shirt-like blouse covering her arms all the way to her wrists, hair in a neatly tied bun and covered by her saree pallu, she looked ascetic and angelic at the same time. These conversations were so different from what she had been used to all her life. They were so open and full of possibilities.

Sagunabai's own story was rather unfortunate.[49] Born in Dhankabadi village near Naigaon, Satara, she was a victim of child marriage. Within a couple of years of her marriage, she became

49 O. Kashyap, *Guide to the Phule Couple, a Symbol of Love and Compassion, Sagunabai Kshirsagar*, (Forward Press, 2020).

a widow. She was told to wear white and grieve in perpetuity. Saguna had never understood the meaning of marriage and hence did not understand the meaning of widowhood either. But what happened after she was widowed was depressing. There were murmurs that she should be burnt alive on her husband's funeral pyre, like Sati. There were people who wanted her to shave her head.

One day, as she was walking aimlessly on the streets, wondering what to do with her life, a local missionary named Father John, who lived close to her cousin Govindrao's house, took pity on her. Father John and his wife Mary ran a shelter for orphans and they needed someone to work there. Saguna gladly joined his cause. Soon enough, Father John learnt that Sagunabai had a keen and perceptive mind. She was also roped in to take care of his son James John, who was almost Jyotirao's age. Working alongside this family, Sagunabai was exposed to a whole new world of books, newspapers, conversations and ideas. She discovered that she had a hunger for learning.

Meanwhile, she got to know that Govindrao's wife Chimnabai had died early. Govindrao sold flowers for a living and did not have the time or the energy to raise his children. He did not want to get married again either. Stuck with a crying infant, Jyoti, his plight was pitiable.

Saguna, who was already taking care of so many orphaned children, felt that she could play a mother's role in Jyoti's life too.

As he grew older, she relayed all that she learnt from Father John to Jyoti, bringing him books and pictures and making him aware of what was happening all over the world. She introduced him to literature, to the writings of great men and women. She told him about science and technology. Jyoti's world widened like never before.

Jyoti's mindset would never have been what it was if not for Saguna.

'Employ your time in improving yourself by other men's writings, so that you shall gain easily what others have laboured hard for.'

—Socrates

Facing page: Fatima Sheikh teaching at the school for girls. Reproduced with permission from Azad Publishers.

PART 2

THE FIRE

Section 5

Sagunabai's Matchmaking Skills

Saguna, intrigued by what she had overheard about Savitri at the Mitchell's home, wanted to find out more about the girl as she felt that Savitri would be a good match for her nephew Jyoti. She went on to cleverly mastermind their marriage. She played a pivotal role in the social revolution, thanks to three things, namely, her motherly love for Jyoti, her resolve that other widows must not go through what she had to endure and finally, her interactions with missionaries, which liberated her mind.

15

Does Our Dharma Allow Education?

The year was 1840. One evening, as Saguna returned home from the Mitchells' house, she had many things on her mind. The first one being that she wanted to resolve a long-standing fight between her brother Govindrao and his son Jyoti.

In a way, she had been responsible for the skirmish between the two. A couple of months ago, Govindrao had wanted Jyoti to join his business—the gardening trade. When he shared this with Saguna, she was worried that Govindrao would make Jyoti discontinue his schooling. So, she offered him her perspective.

'Bhau, Father John tells me that many farmers are exploited because they don't know how to keep accounts properly. So, I think it is a very good idea for Jyoti to join you. He must learn mathematics so he can keep the books and manage the money and prevent the Brahmin accountants from hoodwinking you.'

Govindrao looked at Saguna incredulously, 'Hasn't Krishnaji been keeping accounts properly?'

Saguna insisted, 'Yes he has, Bhau. But the Brahmins don't like Jyoti because he keeps questioning everything they say. If they decide not to give him business, he will have to mingle with the English to earn his livelihood. He has to be able to talk to them in their language and learn how to do accounts. To do this, he must continue in the school.'

Govindrao found nothing objectionable in this and agreed to send Jyoti to a proper English school. However, as soon as he enrolled Jyoti into a Mission school, the Brahmins were upset.

Krishnaji told him, 'Hindu dharma does not allow the lower castes to get an education. If you educate him, seven of your generations will rot in hell.'

This prospect scared Govindrao, who immediately removed Jyoti from the school. Saguna was incensed by Krishnaji's mischief. She believed that Jyoti had a bright future and did not want to see it go to waste. So, she appealed to Officer Lizzit and Persian scholar Munshi Gafar Baig, a respected man who lived in the neighbourhood, to talk to Govindrao and make him see reason. Her appeals brought Baig Sahab home to meet Govindrao.

'Govindrao, why are you removing Jyoti from school? What is the connection between caste and education?'

Govindrao seemed confused. 'Baig Sahab, I owe so much to the Brahmins. How can I go against them? My father Shetiba squandered all our wealth. I have had to work hard and even though we are part of the Mali community and ranked as Shudras, I believe that my work has given us a respectable position among the Maratha Kunbi. It was the Maratha Peshwa Bajirao II who engaged me to supply the court in Poona with flowers for the numerous rituals and ceremonies.[50] Bajirao then

---

50 Rosalind O'Hanlon, *Caste, Conflict and Ideology: Mahatma Jotirao Phule and Low Caste Protest in Nineteenth Century Western India*, (Cambridge University Press, 1985).

conferred thirty-five acres of inam land to us. Our family is well placed, and we owe our allegiance to the Peshwa. Even today, I supply flowers to all the Brahmins who need them for puja in the temples and in people's homes. Our survival depends on their benevolence.'

Baig could see why Govindrao looked pained. 'Don't forget your own hard work, Govind. True, the Brahmins have supported you. But times are changing.'

Govindrao raised his hands. 'Maybe. But if the Brahmins think that Jyoti must not study further, are they wrong? How will my flower business survive without their support?'

'In what way is Jyoti threatening your survival?'

'Baig Sahab, everyone says that if I send my Jyoti to the Mission school, they will convert him to Christianity,' said Govindrao, worry writ over his face. 'Then my business will also shut down.'

Baig Sahab smiled. 'If that is the case, then why are large numbers of Brahmins sending their children to Mission schools?'

Govindrao was stumped. He realized that it was a mistake to have taken his son out of school.

'You see, they are just upset that Jyoti is taking their seat. But it is not too late. Jyoti is still a child, just thirteen. With Officer Lizzit's help, we can get him admission in a good Mission school,' Baig said.

Govindrao was a pliable man. 'Very well, Baig Sahab. But I have one condition. I will allow Jyoti to go back to school only if he agrees to get married. He is very immature, he keeps picking arguments with everyone. Marriage will sober him, make him more mature.'

Saguna had witnessed this exchange. Govindrao asked her to convey his decision to Jyoti. She was happy to have resolved this stand-off between father and son. When she shared the conversation with Jyoti, he flatly refused to get married. But Saguna knew that he wanted to study so badly, he would eventually agree. Now, the problem was to find a suitable girl.

Precisely why Saguna had been so interested in the conversation at the Mitchells' house over luncheon about the patil of Naigaon and his daughter. She thought that the girl Lizzit had referred to might be just right for Jyoti.

That night, she told Govindrao that the patil of Naigaon, Khandoji Nevse, had a daughter of marriageable age. He was a well-liked leader, respected by the English and locals alike, and a man of dharma. Such an alliance would be ideal.

She conveniently left out the part that Savitri was keen to study and that the little girl too had a rebellious nature.

The village patil was always a respected figure, and Govindrao was certain that the match would meet the standards he had always hoped for, for his son's alliance. More importantly, since the patil's daughter was Saguna's choice, he was certain that Jyoti would agree. Promptly, he requested Lizzit to send a letter to Khandoji about his desire to visit their home.

16

Savitri Receives a Proposal

It was the auspicious day of Akshay Tritiya, when the entire village welcomed the return of the idol of Ambe Ma, the village deity. According to tradition, the idol was taken by a procession of devotees on Chaitra Ekadashi to visit Tuljapur and bought back on this day. This 'yatra' or journey was supposed to bring good fortune to the village.

Khandoji Nevse Patil was getting dressed for an afternoon of revelry. His sons Sindhuji, Sakharam and Shripati were also getting ready.

Suddenly, Khandoji felt someone tugging at his dhoti. It was Savitri, his only daughter. And she was all set to trouble her father, because she was feeling lonely and bored.

Savitri now spent most of her days by herself. Mukta wasn't allowed to be with her any more as Gajri felt that Savitri's boldness was a bad influence on her. So Savitri found ways to entertain herself. She was fond of making houses for her dolls.

She would lay sticks down in a criss-cross pattern, then place stones at the vertices. She would then dig some sticks into the ground, drape a piece of cloth over them and make a small tent for her dolls. Her intelligence was visible in the way she planned the balance of the tent and the complex designs she drew in the soil and in her drawing book.

Savitri was petulant. 'Baba, teach me a new song.'

Khandoji said affectionately, 'Laadki,[51] I will surely teach you. But don't we have to rush to the temple today?'

Savitri protested, 'Every afternoon, you promise to teach me in the evening. And every evening, you say you will teach me the next day. You have time to solve the problems of everyone in the village. What about me?'

She sat down with her arms folded in childlike anguish.

Khandoji started singing,

'Vikat vaat vahivaat nasavi, dhopat marga sodu nako
Sansaramadhi ais aapla, ugaach bhatkat firoo nako.'
(When times get tough, don't leave the righteous path
Recognize where you belong, don't wander around.)

Savitri stood up and repeated after him flawlessly, holding her skirt and swaying from side to side.

Khandoji continued.

'Chal salaspan dharuni nikhalas, khotya bola bolu nako
Angi namrata sada asaavi, raag kunavar dharu nako.'
(Laziness is harmful, so are lies;
Be humble and never lose your temper.)

---

51 Laadki is a term of endearment.

Savitri repeated after him, not missing a single word.

'Baba, who wrote this poem?'

'It's not a poem, it's a phatka. Anant Phandi Sahab,[52] a famous poet and performer of ballads, wrote it.'

Savitri started prancing around the room happily, reciting the entire poem. Just then her mother Laxmi entered, upset with both Savitri and Khandoji.

'Baba and Laadki are singing, even though the whole village waits!' she scolded.

Laxmi was right. There would be celebrations at the Ambe Mata temple with musicians playing the dhol and lejhim. Powadas, traditional Marathi ballads glorifying God or a venerated personality,[53] would be sung, followed by dancing, festivities and the customary prasad. The entire village would come alive with religious fervour.

Khandoji's presence to welcome the procession was important.

Laxmi said firmly, 'Let us go. And please stop teaching Savitri new things. How many times have I told you that she has crossed eight years of age? You need to find a groom for her.'

Savitri looked at her father with fearful eyes and shook her head vigorously.

Khandoji smiled.

Savitri implored, 'Baba, I want to learn how to read and write!'

Laxmi retorted, 'Then nobody will marry you.'

'I don't want to get married,' cried Savitri.

Khandoji put a hand on Savitri's indignant head and said, 'I will find the right person for my Savitri. She just repeated the

---

52 Anant Phandi's (born 1744) real name was Anant Gholap and he was traditionally from a family of goldsmiths.

53 Jyotirao Phule wrote several powadas about Chhatrapati Shivaji.

entire phatka without missing a single word! How can I get her married to someone who will not appreciate her intelligence?'

Savitri looked at her father with pride. Khandoji was a highly respected man. It was believed that in the fifteenth century, Khandoji's forefathers had fought in the great Talikota war, a decisive war in the sixteenth century, that had changed the power equations in the Deccan. They were hence inamdars—those who had received land from the kings of yore for their bravery. A hardworking leader of the Mali caste, Khandoji himself was a farmer. Savitri knew that she was the apple of his eye.

Meanwhile, Laxmi was worried sick about Savitri. In her heart, she knew that Khandoji was right about Savitri's mind. Savitri had an exceptional memory. She was a curious and happy child. She sat with her brothers whenever they studied and had already learnt the alphabet. She could tell the time accurately, recite poems and songs ad lib and was quick to grasp anything new. As a mother, Laxmi was anxious to get Savitri married before she learnt too much for her own good. The only path to happiness for Savitri was a husband who lived and would let her live too. Engrossed in such thoughts, the Patil family left to receive the revellers.

The very next day, Khandoji received a letter by post. Gangal Kaka, who was once again tasked with reading out the letter to Khandoji, was extremely happy with its contents. What would he not give for this pesky child Savitri to leave the village! So he happily announced that a marriage proposal had come for Savitri. Patwardhan immediately said that some form of annadanam would be due soon.

Khandoji was overjoyed. He sent an invitation for Govind to visit their house and meet them. In a couple of days, Jyoti's older brother Rajaram and Govindrao set off for Naigaon to meet Savitri.

Saguna and Jyoti were alone in their home. They sat down to talk. Jyoti demanded, 'Aau, why have you got Baba all excited about my marriage? I want to study, become capable.'

Saguna patted his back. 'Of course you will. This girl is just right for you. Don't you have faith in me?'

'You're the only one I have faith in right now. I am shocked at how gullible Baba is.'

Saguna smiled. 'Many things shock me too, Jyoti. When a Mahar fights for the British army against the Peshwa, doesn't it surprise you?'

Jyoti contemplated this. 'Aau, they are being loyal to their salt, not their soil. It is the Britishers who pay them. Our rajas and maharajas were lost in their own pleasures. They didn't care about their people, and so the people stopped caring about them.'

Saguna demanded, 'How can you be sure that the Britishers care? I agree that the Britishers we have met—Lizzit Sahab, Mrs Mitchell, Father John—are kind people. But every so often, I hear about the atrocities committed by the British. I'm not sure that everything is as it seems.'

'You're right, Aau. But all around us, they're the ones opening schools. The Brahmins just beat Moligude to death because he wasn't wearing a pot around his neck and Purohitji stepped on his sweat. They are the worst. Anyone is better than them.' Jyoti's hatred was clear.

Saguna tried to calm him. 'It seems that way today, but the idea that the British, who have no relation to us, have suddenly started caring for us, doesn't make sense to me.'

Jyoti thought for a minute. 'What do our poor people even have to give them, Aau? What could they possibly want?'

Saguna spoke, 'I wish I knew. But here's what I do know, Jyoti. I think you have a fine mind that can help people. I want you to study the literature of Gautama Buddha, Guru Nanak, Sant

Kabir and other such great personages so you understand the values that we must all cherish. You will see that when a person is deprived of education, they cannot see their place in society and their worth. They become dependent and then they get exploited. This is the plight not just of widows but of Shudras, Atishudras and women in general. Unless the masses are educated there will always be the oppressor and the oppressed. Jyoti, I want you to create a society free of all exploitation.'

'Aau, you never told me this before. You are a revolutionary yourself,' Jyoti teased.

Saguna's intense eyes were honest. 'Listening to Father John and spending time with women like Mrs Mitchell has opened my eyes. She picks up any book she wants to, reads and understands it. I wish I could be like her!'

'Aau, I will teach you myself.'

'Yes of course you will, Jyoti. But Mrs Mitchell has also agreed to teach me. Earlier, these Brahmins threatened me that my husband would die if I tried to educate myself. At least that fear can't hold me back now! My husband has died and hopefully is in heaven.' Saguna laughed at her own misery.

17

Jyotirao's Awakening

Finally, the day came when Savitri and Jyoti got married. It was 1840. Jyoti was thirteen and Savitri was just nine. Khandoji's happiness knew no bounds that Savitri had found a husband who could handle her curiosity.

Munshi Gafar Baig enrolled Jyotirao in the government English school in Budhwarwada, after arranging a letter of permission from the Collector's office, no less. This was in 1842 and Govindrao did not object.

With his mind now fired up by Saguna's ideals, Jyoti's life would be transformed even further in the school. He learnt English and was exposed to the ideas of Thomas Paine and Socrates.

His young bride Savitri took some time to settle into the new household. She was mindful of the respect she had to show Govindrao, her father-in-law. Govindrao was thrilled to have her bubbly presence in the house.

With Jyoti, one could say that Savitri was her usual transparent self from day one! One of the couple's earliest conversations involved Jyoti reassuring her that no one would die if she learnt how to read and write. When Saguna also assured her of this, Savitri took to learning like a fish takes to water. Her curiosity was so intense that Jyoti taught her the Marathi alphabet. With a slate and chalk hidden in her room, Savitri progressed from the alphabet to words and from words to simple sentences. Jyoti was extremely happy that he had found a life partner who was keen to learn.

He would share with her his experiences in school, which was a different world from that of Poona society at large. Unlike the earlier Marathi-medium school, the government English school encouraged the sharing of opinions. He was exposed to a healthy and heterogenous learning environment, and there were a few Mahar and Mang students in the school as well. Everyone was encouraged to debate with each other about the social and ritualistic nature of caste. This was a freedom unlike anything Jyoti had seen before. There were no diktats that one had to follow; everyone was encouraged to have a point of view. Such debates shaped Jyoti's mind.

Thomas Paine's *Age of Reason*[54] exercised a particular influence on Jyoti and his views were forceful. Paine says in his book: 'I believe in one God, and no more; and I hope for happiness beyond this life. I believe in the equality of man; and I believe that religious duties consist in doing justice, loving mercy, and endeavouring to make our fellow-creatures happy.'

Further, Thomas Paine insisted that there was no need for an intermediary to worship God.

---

54 Published in three parts (1794, 1795, 1807), Thomas Paine's *Age of Reason* reflects his belief that a significant religious upheaval would follow in the wake of the American and French Revolutions.

On the subject of religion, Jyoti's young friends had varied opinions. In an essay written years later, Laxmanrao Devrao Thosar,[55] son of Jyoti's lifelong friend Devrao Krishna Thosar,[56] recalls that his father was given the New Testament as a present when he wrote a good essay in school. This could be seen as a subtle attempt to indoctrinate him.

Jyoti's childhood friend and colleague Moro Vitthal Walvekar recalls that 'he had found most striking in the missionary teaching, the urge to reform Hindoo society and to do good to his countrymen'.[57]

Another candid narration comes from Krishnarao Arjun Keluskar, Jyoti's colleague and friend. He describes his impression of Jyoti's early religious attitudes as follows: 'Many educated people at that time thought that the Christian religion was better than their own religion, and some people even became Christian themselves. But Jyotirao and his friends did not become Christians.'

Exposed to multiple ideas, Jyotirao came to the conclusion that progress was connected more deeply to education than anything else. And that, independent of one's religious beliefs, education can be a leveller for civilization at large. Hence, Jyotirao and his friends did not feel the need to change their own religion.

---

55 Hari Narke (ed.), *Aamhi Pahilele Jyotirao Phule*, eleventh edition, (Mahatma Jyotirao Phule Charitra Sadhane Prakashan Samiti, 2018).

56 Devrao Krishna Thosar joined the police and worked for the improvement of the police force in Poona. His son Laxmanrao eventually became friends with Yashwant, the adopted son of Jyoti and Savitri.

57 Rosalind O'Hanlon, *Caste, Conflict and Ideology: Mahatma Jotirao Phule and Low Caste Protest in Nineteenth Century Western India*, (Cambridge University Press, 1985).

He continued to to teach Marathi to both Sagunabai and Savitri at home. Often, his friends Sakharam Yashwant Paranjpe and Keshav Shivram Bhawalkar[58] also helped in this process. Jyoti completed his formal secondary education in the year 1847.[59]

It was around this time that he met Sadashiv Ballal Govande, a Brahmin who would remain a friend and associate throughout his life. Sadashiv's wife, Saraswati Govande, would play a major part in the revolution too. The willing participation of a handful of Brahmins in uprooting the hegemony of their fellows, was one of the most unique aspects of India's socio-cultural revolution in the nineteenth century, led by the Phule couple.

58 Keshav Shivram Bhawalkar was a Brahmin and a government teacher at the Marathi School. He was also a member of the Paramhansa Sabha. A separate biography of Keshav Shivam Bhawalkar is available in Marathi.

59 Dhananjay Keer, *Mahatma Jyotirao Phuley*, (Popular Prakashan, 2012).

'The British occupation differs fundamentally from the Muslim conquest of India. While the intellectual impact of Islam had been marginal, British rule opened the eyes of the intelligentsia to a new and exciting range of social values and political objectives, and it convinced the educated community of the advantages of representative government and popular democracy. Through promoting a change in the intellectual climate, the British Government had cleared the way for the political emancipation of the country.'

—Gopal Hari Deshmukh[60]

---

60 Gopal Hari Deshmukh, also known as Lokhitwadi, was a product of Western education. He was a great social reformer and rational thinker, who encouraged people to be self-sufficient and seek Western education. From 1848 onwards, he published a series of short articles on religious, social, political, economic and educational topics in the periodical *Prabhakar*. He also contributed to the development of a liberal political philosophy. He was primarily inspired by the dynastic lineage of Jeremy Bentham, James Mill and John Stuart Mill. Later, he had differences of opinion with Jyotirao over the Prarthana Samaj. Quote from D.A. Low (ed.), *Soundings in Modern South Asian History*, (University of California Press, 1968).

Section 6

A Tale of Two Sisters

It is time now for Savitri to meet Fatima, thanks to the work of missionaries. Brian Holmes[61] has famously pointed out the mystifying mix of the British influence succinctly as follows, 'The traders usually arrived first, then the missionaries.'

Some versions of published literature claim that Fatima Sheikh and Savitri Phule first met at their teacher Cynthia Farrar's school in Ahmednagar. Other versions say that they first met at Mrs Mitchell's Normal School[62]—a teacher training school for women teachers—in Poona, where both of them studied. We are going with the latter version.

The other thing to note is that during the colonial occupation of India, in the 1840s, cameras first made their appearance. It served British interests to take pictures of India and send them back to England to prove that India was a land desperately in need of intervention and that the British occupation was indeed a favour to the poor Indians.

---

61 Brian Holmes (ed.), *Educational Policy and the Mission Schools, Case Studies from the British Empire*, (Routledge, 1967).

62 Normal Schools derive their name from the French phrase *école normale.* These teacher-training institutions, the first of which was established in France by the Brothers of the Christian Schools in 1685, were intended to set a pattern and establish a 'norm' after which all other schools would be modelled.

18

Savitri's Education and the Meeting with Fatima

Within the first year of Jyoti and Savitri's marriage, Saguna was delighted to see that the two got along well; they behaved like friends discovering new learnings together. She started taking Savitri with her to Father John's orphanage as well as Mrs Mitchell's home.

Mrs Mitchell had started a Normal School[63] in a colony, also called 'wada' in the local language, belonging to a Mr Chhabildas. These Normal Schools eventually played a massive role in the

63 The female Normal School was a part of the influential policy intervention by English educational and social reformer Mary Carpenter (1807–1877) who advocated that the government must invest in teacher training, as reported in Antoinette Burton, *Burdens of History: British Feminists, Indian Women and Imperial Culture, 1865-1915*, (University of North Carolina Press, 2000).

transformation of the lives of women in what is today western India.[64]

Mrs Mitchell was constantly looking for young ladies to train. So, when she saw both Saguna and Savitri poring over the pictures in books and newspapers, she asked them how much they had studied. Saguna told her that Jyotirao and his friends were teaching them how to read and write Marathi.

As they'd had no formal schooling, Mrs Mitchell had to find a way to integrate them into the system. So, she made both of them take an exam and gave them some time to prepare. She was overjoyed when they cleared it. In 1843, she admitted both Sagunabai and Savitri into the Normal School so they could be trained as elementary schoolteachers.

When they began to attend the sessions, Mrs Mitchell introduced them to a few other students in the class. One of these was Fatima Sheikh. She had a bright smile and a purposeful expression.

'Meet one of your fellow students, Fatima. I met her because her brother Usman supplies cloth to one of our friends, and he told me about her desire to learn. Fatima also embroiders very well.'

Fatima said excitedly, 'Mitchell madam is kind. My mother was my first teacher. But I've realized now that work is the greatest teacher. Every time a memsahib wants something specific, I learn something new. Mrs Brown has taught me many new embroidery and appliqué styles.'

---

64 The report of the Indian Education Commission, Bombay Provincial Committee, Evidence and Memorials II states that a total of thirty-four teachers were trained in such schools—seventeen Brahmins, twelve Kunbis, two Sonars, one Pardeshi, one Jew and one Muslim (pp. 382–388).

The pace at which Fatima spoke was a window into her heart. The impetuousness of her childhood, indulged by her protective brother, had given way to an enthusiasm for learning. Fatima spoke with the excitement of one who trusts the whole wide world. Saguna was so taken in by Fatima's artlessness that she hugged her warmly. Savitri and Fatima smiled at each other. Savitri's deportment too was open and warm. Fatima naturally gravitated towards her. Both of them were just twelve years old.

Mrs Mitchell continued, 'Do you know, Savitri, Fatima is a very special name. The great Prophet Mohammed, the founder of Islam, had four daughters—his youngest daughter's name was Fatima. It was Fatima who witnessed the emergence of the great principles of Islam in her father's house. Fatima was a great believer in kindness.'

'Arre wah! What a special name indeed. Kindness and compassion are common to all religions. I want to meet your brother Usman Bhai. Your journey to this school and your work, I'm sure, has been as difficult as ours. The fact that your innocence has been preserved through it all shows what kind of a man your brother is. Just like my Shetji.'

Curious, Fatima asked, 'Who is Shetji?'

'My husband,' said Savitri. 'He believes that girls should get educated and has taught me himself.'

Mrs Mitchell shared that Usman had studied in the same school as Jyoti for a while and that the two young men knew each other.

Fatima jumped with excitement. 'You must meet Usman Bhaijaan, Savitri Aapa. He is my world!'

Over time, Savitri and Fatima got to know each other very well. Savitri's own childhood had been relatively secure, and she marvelled at Usman and Fatima's stressful migratory experiences and the hardships that they had had to overcome.

Mrs Mitchell taught Fatima, Savitri and Saguna the basics of English language, reading and writing. What also helped Fatima and Savitri's friendship blossom was that Saguna, having settled Jyoti into marriage, felt she had discharged her duties towards him. She started to spend more time at Father John's orphanage. In her absence, Savitri, a friendly person by nature, started seeking out Fatima's company.

Over time, Saguna was given more and more responsibilities and even moved to the orphanage to live with the children. In many ways, Saguna learnt more by talking to and being around Father John, and the extent of her learning was beyond any certificate or degree.

Jyoti had also finished his education. Not only was he helping Govindrao with the business, but he was also constantly looking for new contracting opportunities offered by the British Government.

19

Ruchi Vahini and Purohitji

Soon enough, Savitri Phule completed her elementary-level teacher-training course with Mrs Mitchell. It is believed that she was the first Indian[65] woman to do so. Mrs Mitchell and Fatima visited Savitri's house to give her the certificate of completion.

'Savitri, here is your certificate of completion of the elementary-level teacher training.'

Savitri was happy at first and took the certificate from Mrs Mitchell with glee. Then she said ruefully, 'This certificate is useless if I cannot train others.'

Mrs Mitchell offered, 'You can start teaching at a basic level in the Mission schools. Fatima will complete her course soon as well. Both of you are welcome to teach there.'

65 Outlook Web Desk, 'The Life of India's First Woman Teacher and a Fierce Feminist Icon,' *Outlook India*, 3 January 2023.

Savitri responded thoughtfully, 'Mitchell madam, Shetji and I want to teach other lower-caste local girls. That is why we have set out on this path.'

Fatima nodded. 'Aapa, you and I both will teach girls from every segment of society.'

Mrs Mitchell smiled. 'You have taken the first step. God will show you the way, my child.'

As Fatima and Mrs Mitchell were leaving Savitri's house, Fatima saw Ruchi Vahini, wife of Purohitji, the priest of the nearby Vitthala temple. Given her open nature, Fatima excitedly told Ruchi that it was a day of great pride for every Indian woman as her neighbour, Savitri, had become the first woman in India to be trained as a teacher.

'Pride?' wondered Ruchi scornfully.

Fatima's happy revelation was just the kind of gossip that Ruchi needed to stir up trouble. She had always believed that Savitri was up to some mischief. She was never at home, and her husband Jyoti was an abomination to all Brahmins. Ruchi had a daughter of her own—Purnima—whom she kept away from 'dangerous' influences like Savitri. Ruchi personified the adage 'an idle mind is the devil's workshop'. She was staunchly opposed to any digression from custom and loved to gossip. That night, she told her husband Purohitji that Govindrao's daughter-in-law Savitri had completed a course of study and intended to teach other girls as well. And that the infernal, ultra-liberated Muslim girl Fatima was in cahoots with her.

Purohitji confronted Govindrao the next morning.

'Govindrao, you better stop supplying flowers to the temples. Your son was always a headache. Now your daughter-in-law it seems is a step ahead. Did you know that she has been learning how to read and write English at Mrs Mitchell's Normal School?'

Govindrao was aghast. 'I had no idea.'

'Arre moorkh, you ignorant man, do you not know what is happening in your own house? Go and ask your daughter-in-law. Then come and talk to me!'

Meanwhile, Ruchi visited Savitri. She asked her if she could help her write *'Om Ganeshaya Namaha'* on her doorstep as Purohitji was away from home. Savitri happily consented and accompanied Ruchi to her house to do the needful.

Just as she was writing out the phrase, Ruchi slyly fetched Govindrao and showed him what Savitri was up to.

'Savitri! What are you doing?' he exclaimed.

Savitri was shocked to see Ruchi standing behind Govindrao.

'Ruchi Vahini asked for my help. I was helping her, Baba.'

'How? By learning how to read and write behind my back? By destroying our dharma? By shutting down my business of supplying flowers to all the temples?'

Savitri realized that this was exactly what Ruchi Vahini wanted. So she remained calm, even as Ruchi smirked at her.

'Baba, let us go home and talk.'

'There is nothing to talk about,' Govindrao fumed.

Fortunately, he was so angry that he turned around and went back to his farm. Savitri had some time to think about what to do next. That evening, when Jyoti returned home, he was excited about a new book he had read, *The Writings* by George Washington.[66]

---

66 Phule's biographers give the first direct comments on the development of Phule's ideas. In Dhananjay Keer's *Mahatma Jyotirao Phuley*, published by Popular Prakashan in 2012, the biographer suggests that twenty-year-old Phule and his friends are said to have been fired with ideas of liberating their country from foreign rule by their reading of the lives of Shivaji and George Washington, and of the work of Thomas Paine, and by the influence of anti-British Brahmins.

Jyotirao wanted to share his thoughts on the book with his wife. 'Savitri, I have never read such a wide range of experiences narrated by one man. George Washington freed a country called America from the British. In the book, he talks about being goal-oriented. He understands his own worth but is always modest in describing his accomplishments. He made many decisions—instantly if the situation demanded speed, or slowly after deep and thoughtful examination. His letters display his many skills, from farming and experimenting with soils to political commentary and participation, as well as public works and their financing. He is quite spectacular!'

Savitri heard him out and then, after Jyoti's excitement subsided, she narrated the events of the afternoon to him.

'Baba is upset that I went to Mrs Mitchell's school behind his back,' she said gently.

Just then Govindrao returned home. He sat down and hit his forehead sharply with his palm thrice, shaking his head in chagrin.

'Jyoti, Savitri, I really don't know how to explain right and wrong to you any more. The Brahmins have told me that they don't want me to supply flowers to them because both of you are a threat to dharma,' he said, his voice tired.

Jyoti was in no mood for this. 'Baba, we have had this discussion so many times. How can education be a threat to dharma?'

'Jyoti, I am not such a great man that I can question Maha Pandit Bhattji. I am a simple man who earns his livelihood by selling flowers. I am not a revolutionary.'

Savitri spoke before Jyoti could. 'Baba, my mistake is not that I got educated. My mistake is that I did it behind your back. That you had to hear about it from others. I'm sorry about that.'

They were interrupted by Ruchi knocking on their front door. One wonders how long she might have been eavesdropping on this conversation.

As she entered, she declared, 'Jyoti, Purohitji has informed Maha Pandit Bhattji about your wife's wild ways. The Peshwa has summoned you tomorrow. You can share all your great knowledge in his darbar, about how managing your household is not enough for your wife. She has other thirsts and desires.'

So saying, she shook her head and stormed out.

Jyoti was about to retaliate, but Savitri held his hand.

'Reserve your energy for the Peshwa tomorrow. People like Ruchi Vahini don't matter.'

Govindrao sat down, melancholy and dejected. Was Jyoti going to make an enemy of the Peshwa too? Seeing his state, Jyoti and Savitri decided to spare Govindrao any further arguments. Instead, Jyoti took pen and paper and sat down to write out the defence he would present to the Peshwa.

Meanwhile, both Purohitji and Maha Pandit Bhatt had great expectations from the Peshwa's meeting with Jyoti. They believed that the Peshwa would punish Jyoti for daring to educate his wife.

Talk that Jyoti had been summoned to the Peshwa's darbar spread like wildfire. His friend Sakharam Yashwant Paranjpe in particular was worried for Jyoti. Like many Marathas, Sakharam's family had been historically loyal to the Peshwas. To their mind, the Peshwa was yet a figure of absolute authority.

20

Usman Builds a Successful Business

Usman Sheikh's textile shop was a wonderful mess.

There were rolls of fabric, embroidery patches, swatches and cut pieces lying everywhere, and yet Usman seemed to know exactly where each item was. Muhasibji, his reliable accountant, was sitting in his usual place at the shop. One wondered whether Muhasibji even answered nature's call, such was his loyalty to Usman and his perennial presence at the shop.

One evening, as was his habit, Munshi Gafar Baig dropped in for a chat. Muhasibji was happy to see Baig Sahab because he always recited poetry and had news.

'*Usman, sab khairiyat* (all well)?'

'Yes, Baig Chacha. Will you have some tea?' offered Usman.

'Yes, Usman. A good cup of tea and happy conversations are all we truly have. Otherwise, as Urdu poet Mir Mohammad Taqi wrote,

"Subah hoti hai shaam hoti hai
Umra yoonhi tamaam hoti hai."
(With each morning and evening,
Life passes us by.)'

'Waah Baig Sahab, waah!' exclaimed Muhasibji.

'Thank you, Muhasibji. Usman, Father John wants you to show him some new fabric for the children. He's preparing them for a programme.'

'Sometimes I wonder how the Angrez even got here,' mused Muhasibji. One couldn't make out if he was speaking in context or absentmindedly.

'They are very smart people. First, they took Bengal, then Bihar, Orissa, Awadh and now the Maratha kingdom. They have taken over everything!' Usman said ruefully.

'But how is it their fault?' asked Baig. 'There is no unity among our own people. Would the British have defeated the nawab of Bengal, Siraj ud-Daulah, in the Battle of Plassey if Mir Jaffar, his own commander, had not been so greedy and betrayed him to the British? The fact is that if not the British, then the French might have ruled us. If the French government had not recalled Joseph-François Dupleix, the governor-general of their territories in India, we might have been answerable to the French East India company instead of the British East India company. These foreign powers are all enticed by our vast wealth.'

'Baig Chacha, I am not able to wrap my head around all this. When I meet the British, they seem so affable and kind. It is almost impossible to imagine that they have been playing the divide-and-rule game and are actually sinister,' said Usman.

Baig nodded. 'Usman, the fight is over and the British have won. They have defeated the Marathas fair and square. Not just our Peshwa, but the Gaekwads of Baroda, the Scindias at

Gwalior, the Holkars of Indore and the Bhonsles of Nagpur, all were fighting among each other, blind to the real danger from the British. Now, it is their time to govern and maintain peace. You see their kind face because they are consolidating their power.'

Muhasibji stepped in with a question, 'How come no one saw this coming?'

'Let me tell you a story. There is an Angrez officer named Wellesley Sahab. He devised a very smart scheme called the subsidiary alliance. He saw that two neighbouring kings did not trust each other. So, he offered protection to both of them for money. And our foolish rajas paid the Angrez to rule over their own houses.'

Muhasibji shook his head in disbelief. 'Don't the rajas realize what is happening?'

'Yes, they do. And the self-respecting ones fight. Tipu Sultan, the proud king of Mysore, saw that the British were maintaining an army at the expense of the Indian kings. He tried to get French help to overthrow them, but the British defeated Tipu before the French help came.'

'But Baig Sahab, there has to be some end to this,' said Muhasibji hopefully.

'The end will come. It is natural. I can only quote Mir Sahab,

"Jis sar ko ghurur aaj hai yan taj-wari ka
kal us pe yahin shor hai phir nauhagari ka."[67]
(Rulers blinded by pride
Soon fall by the wayside.)'

---

67 Read the full miriyaat by Meer Taqi Meer at https://www.rekhta.org/miiriyaat/jis-sar-ko-guruur-aaj-hai-yaan-taaj-varii-kaa-meer-taqi-meer-miiriyaat

Just then Jyoti's friend Sakharam entered the shop. He seemed disturbed. After greeting everyone he said to Baig Sahab, 'The Peshwa has summoned Jyoti for a hearing!'

'Sakharam, don't worry. We were just talking about the Peshwa. He does not have any real powers now. The Brahmins who are instigating the Peshwa against Jyoti probably don't realize that. You don't have to worry about Jyoti,' counselled Usman.

Sakharam was not convinced. 'Baig Sahab, perhaps you can make Usman understand. Since childhood, we have been taught that the Peshwa controls our destiny. One day, these Angrez will go away. The Peshwas will remain our true rulers. What will happen to Jyoti then?'

'Sakharam, the British are going nowhere. They are here to loot, like Janaab Cortes of Spain looted Mexico. The Peshwas are not coming back to power!'

Muhasibji felt a chill down his spine on hearing the finality of Baig Sahab's words.

Baig continued, 'Remember that the Angrez are ruthless. They don't even spare their own. There was an Englishman by the name of James Augustus Hicky who started a newspaper in 1780 called *Hicky's Bengal Gazette.* It was printed every Saturday. Initially, it was meant as a publication for British readers, but Hicky Sahab got too big for his boots. He started talking about corruption and scandal among the British. When Warren Hastings, the first governor-general of Bengal, stationed troops in the capital of the neighbouring state of Berar to conquer the territory, Hicky called it an "illegal war of conquest". He also accused Hastings of being despotic and disgraceful, bent on conquering all of India. Within two years, in March 1782, Hastings shut down Hicky's newspaper.'

'Then why would the Angrez support Jyoti? Surely the education that he's pushing for is making all of us more aware,' quizzed Usman.

Baig nodded, 'I agree. In his own way, Jyoti is sowing the seeds for an eventual revolt against the Angrez. But they are too short-sighted to see it right now. They feel that Jyoti's efforts to educate the masses will get them cheap labour to fill administrative positions. Jyoti is also creating a local groundswell against the Brahmins, who want to keep all the jobs and dictate terms to the British. If there's one thing we know about the British in India, it's that they don't like being dictated to!'

'So the British are helping Jyoti so that they get cheap labour?' asked Sakharam.

'Whatever it is, he serves their purpose right now. One day, he won't. That day, they won't support him either,' mused Baig.

This was an entirely different point of view for all of them. As he saw their serious faces, Baig Sahab changed the topic, 'Arre Usman, where is Fatima Bibi? She normally has her own point of view during our conversations.'

'Fatima has not one point of view but ten! There is a new guest at Lady Falkland's house. She has gone there with some lengths of fabric,' Usman responded.

Sakharam smiled, but he couldn't help worrying about what fate had in store for Jyotirao at the Peshwa's darbar.

21

The Peshwa's Darbar

Maha Pandit Bhatt, Purohitji, Ruchi Vahini, Govindrao, Jyoti and Sakharam were present at the Peshwa's darbar at the appointed date and time. A few others had gathered too.

Maha Pandit Bhatt sanctimoniously began the proceedings.

'Peshwa Sahab, meet this boy who is single-handedly destroying our Hindu dharma. Jyotirao Phule is the son of Mali Govindrao Phule, who stands with his hands folded, seeking your mercy.'

The Peshwa looked at Govindrao. 'What is this that I'm hearing? Your daughter-in-law has learnt how to read and write in English? And she wants to teach more people?'

'Not just that, she does not apologize for it either. Since Jyoti was a child, all he has done is insult Purohitji. Not only does he not follow Purohitji's dharmic instructions, but he openly flouts them and insults his own father in the process,' declared Maha Pandit Bhatt.

'Peshwa Sahab, you know that the Manusmriti[68] does not allow the Shudras to receive an education. Also, it clearly says, "Let the husband employ his wife in the collection and expenditure of his wealth, in keeping everything clean, in the fulfilment of religious duties, in the preparation of his food, and in looking after the household utensils." There is no reference to any education for women either!'

The Peshwa addressed Govindrao again, 'Our families have a long association. What have we not done for you! Why is your son treating us with disrespect?'

Jyotirao could no longer bear to see his father under such pressure. 'Peshwa Sahab, I request your permission to speak.'

The Peshwa nodded.

'Our Vedic teachings place women at a higher status than men. Women have been given preference over men in every field, so much so that when taking the name of a god and goddess, the name of the goddess is always placed before that of the god. For example, Sita-Rama, Radhe-Shyama and Gauri-Shankar. We are taught to be more indebted to our mother than our father—maatru devobhava before pitru devobhava.'

Both Purohitji and Maha Pandit Bhatt were not expecting such eloquence from Jyotirao.

Jyotirao continued, 'In our Vedic literature, Gargi is honoured as a great philosopher, a renowned expounder of the Vedas, and is known as Brahmavadini, a person with knowledge of Brahma Vidya. The Rig Veda contains hymns written by twenty-seven women scholars.[69] Of these, the prominent Brahmavadinis are

---

68 The Manusmriti, also known as the Manava-Dharmashastra or Laws of Manu, is one of the many legal texts and constitutions among the many dharmashastras of Hinduism.

69 Dr Jagat K. Motwani, *Discovery of Prehistory Ancient India: Krishna & Radha*, (iUniverse, 2018).

Lopamudra, Ghosha, Gargi and Maitreyi. With such a rich culture of education among goddesses, why are Purohitji and Maha Pandit Bhattji worried that my poor wife is a threat to dharma?'

The Peshwa wasn't prepared for such an elaborate argument. He passed the baton. 'Purohitji, Bhattji, is there anything you have to say?'

Purohit mumbled, 'Peshwa Sahab, he is equating his wife to the goddesses. He is delusional. What can we possibly say?'

'In that case,' said Jyoti, 'let me read out your own Manusmriti to you:

> *"Yatra naryastu pujyante, ramante tatra devata*
> *Yatraihastu na pujyante, sarvastatraphala kriya."*
> (Where women are worshipped, deities reside, and where women are not worshipped or respected, all the good deeds done there become fruitless.)'

The argument, for all practical purposes, was over, and Jyoti had won it decisively!

Ruchi Vahini, who had come dressed in all her finery to see Jyoti being rapped on the knuckles, left in a huff. She did not know what upset her more—the fact that Jyotirao stood up for his wife, or that her own supposedly learned husband Purohitji could not quote appropriate verses in response to Jyotirao's arguments.

Similarly, Govindrao did not know whether to be happy or sad. All his life, he had listened to Purohitji. Today, his own son had quoted the shastras back to the Brahmins.

As for Jyotirao, he had never been worried about meeting the Peshwa.

22

Farrar and Foresight

After the infamous darbar with the Peshwa, the Brahmins left Jyotirao alone for some time. He in turn was determined to become more goal-oriented (as he had read in George Washington's writings) and start a school for the education of girls, Shudras and Atishudras.

One evening, Jyotirao called out to Savitri excitedly as soon as he returned home.

Savitri asked him, 'What is the reason for this big smile?'

'You remember Govande, my classmate from school? He has started working at the judge's office in Ahmednagar. He took me to meet a missionary named Cynthia Farrar who is running a girls' school for the American Marathi Mission. The training she gives there is a step ahead of that at Mrs Mitchell's school.'

This piqued Savitri's curiosity. For a while now, Jyoti and she had harboured a dream of opening schools for the local girls. But she was worried that she may not be qualified enough to teach.

Jyoti continued, 'Farrar[70] madam told me that a woman is the centre of any household. If she is educated, then the situation of the whole family changes drastically. So it is really very sad that we do not educate our wives and girls. And Savitri, would you believe it? Farrar madam has agreed to help us start a school for our girls.'

Savitri could see there was more.

'Farrar madam also said that this was the first time somebody like me, a non-missionary Indian male, has thought of opening schools for girls and women in India. That is why she wants to help our cause. She suggested that we start this mission of women's education from our own home because any reformation that starts from one's own house lasts for a longer time. She also knows that Aau and you are intelligent and clever, and she wants to make you capable so you will be supporters in this great work.'

Savitri was thrilled, but she had her doubts. 'I have always worried about whether I know enough to teach. Whether I can plan lessons. I've been learning for five years now and have had so many teachers; how do I convert what I know into lessons that these little girls who have had no exposure at all will understand? Perhaps Farrar madam can guide me.'

---

70 During this period, missionaries like Cynthia Farrar played a massive role. While single women missionaries in this period either worked as teachers, nurses or doctors, the wives of male missionaries almost invariably undertook work with girls and women. Alongside the development of female education, missionaries regularly denounced the atrocities towards girls and women in India, especially the custom of sati (the burning of wives on their husband's funeral pyres), the treatment of widows, child marriage and temple prostitution. They advocated to British authorities for reform in these areas despite the strong opposition of the local community.

'There is no doubt about it. Farrar madam has agreed to take you on as a student. Once you finish your course with her, you will be completely ready,' Jyoti asserted.

'I will definitely go, but can I take Fatima along with me? She will be a great asset to us.'

It was nothing short of an adventure for a Muslim woman to go to Ahmednagar from Poona for education.[71] But Jyoti saw the wisdom of what Savitri was saying.

'You must take her. I can see that any despotism, whether by the British or the Brahmins, can only be overcome by education. I saw a book in Farrar madam's room called *Rights of Man*[72] by Thomas Paine. I have already read his *Age of Reason*. Paine Sahab says that "the wisdom to govern cannot be inherited". Hence, the hereditary rule of the Peshwas is not feasible. Paine also says that "the aim of every political association is the preservation of the natural and imprescriptible rights of man. These rights are liberty, property, safety and resistance to oppression". We are not free at all, Savitri.'

Savitri was looking at Jyoti in admiration. 'Shetji, perhaps we are not as wrong as the Brahmins think we are when we dream of educating our own people. Let me speak to Fatima.'

Thus, with purpose in their gait and revolution on their minds, Savitri and Fatima set off for Ahmednagar where they were to spend a couple of months training under Cynthia Farrar. They had both appeared for an entrance examination to get admission

---

71 Jill Sperandio, *Pioneering Education for Girls Across the Globe Advocates and Entrepreneurs, (1742-1910)*, (Lexington Books, 2018).

72 *The Rights of Man* (1791) is a philosophical political treatise by English-American political revolutionary and Founding Father Thomas Paine. Comprising thirty-one articles, Paine argues that political revolution is moral, even necessary, when a government fails to protect its citizens' basic rights.

in the teacher-training course and had passed it. The training was immersive.[73]

When Savitri met Cynthia Farrar, she said with folded hands, 'Thank you for agreeing to teach us.'

'It is the Lord's grace, my child.'

Fatima said with her trademark innocence, 'Are we the first teachers you will be training, Farrar madam?'

'You'll be surprised, but no. The Lord's first chastened soul was Gangabai. She was part of our mission in 1824, before my time. She opened a small education centre for women under the American Marathi Mission. She also found support in two English women in Bombay who offered to pay all the expenses of the school.'

Savitri and Fatima glanced at each other in surprise. Savitri said, 'Nobody ever told us about Gangabai.'

'That's probably because just nine months after the school opened, Gangabai succumbed to cholera and went to be with the Lord. As no one could be found to take her place at the time, the school was closed.'

'Thank you for telling us about Gangabai. It seems she was a woman of great courage,' said Fatima, her eyes wide in admiration.

Savitri added, 'With Lord Vitthala's blessings, Fatima and I will complete the work that Gangabai couldn't.'

Farrar smiled. 'You have set a difficult goal, my dear Savitri. Do you know, child, that when I first went from home to home asking girls to join me, I was told by the local Brahmins to first teach the donkeys and then teach the girls.'

There was an uncomfortable silence.

---

73 Jill Sperandio, *Pioneering Education for Girls across the Globe, Advocates and Entrepreneurs, 1742-1910*, (Lexington Books, 2018).

Farrar continued, 'But God's purpose is always greater than man's trifles. The Governor of Bombay and Archbishop Carr helped me keep the faith. They gave me funds raised in England for the education of girls. And I was able to continue my work. What we teach here is reading, writing and arithmetic. You will also have to commit many things to memory, because as teachers, you won't have the luxury to keep referring to books. You have to know the basics. You will also be taught about Christianity, such as learning about the Ten Commandments.'

Neither Fatima nor Savitri had any objection to this. They believed that the teachings of all religions were not very different in essence.

Over the next couple of months, both Fatima and Savitri saw first-hand that Farrar's success was in part due to her approach to teaching. She was confronted with frequent absences when girls were required to remain at home to help their mothers or were withdrawn to be married and sent to their mothers-in-law. 'It was chiefly by gaining the love of her pupils and making it pleasant for them to attend her school'[74] that Miss Farrar could keep them long enough to learn to read and acquire a little knowledge.

Farrar was indeed a compassionate teacher. One day, a large number of girls were in attendance at the school. She asked Savitri, 'Savitri, can you share with us a time when you thought you would never be able to pursue your dream to study?'

Savitri stood up. She had always been confident and had no qualms about speaking in front of a crowd.

'One day, I was playing by myself. The friend I had grown up with, Mukta, was not allowed to play any more. She was told

---

74 Lindley, Susan Hill and Stebner, Eleanor J. *The Westminster Handbook to Women in American Religious History*, (John Knox Press, 2005).

that nobody would marry her if she continued to play. Mukta's mother had also warned her not to be seen with me. I was the village patil's daughter, so even if I picked an argument with people, they would not complain. Besides, I had this habit of sneaking off to the local Brahmin boys' school. I would hide behind a tree and try to learn whatever I could from a distance. Mukta was from a very poor family and she knew that if she were caught with me, the Brahmins would trouble her and her widowed mother to no end.'

Savitri was a great storyteller. Everyone was engrossed.

'That day Gangal Kaka was teaching the alphabet. He had written all the letters on the board. I wanted to copy them, but I didn't have a slate and chalk like the other children, so I wrote in the soil with a stick. Suddenly, Gangal Kaka asked whether anyone remembered the shloka he had taught his students the previous day. I remembered it, but none of the other boys did. In my excitement, I recited it aloud—*vidya dadanti vinayam, vinyad yati patratam* (Knowledge gives discipline, from discipline comes worthiness).

'Gangal Kaka heard me and rushed up to me. He was fuming and screamed, "*Ae patil ki mulgi!*"

'Even though I was scared, I tried my best to look confident. I didn't want to back down because I really enjoyed my escape to school.

'"How dare you come here?" he demanded. "You have contaminated my school. Now I have to wash it with Gangajal!"

'I asked him why, and he said, "Because you are a girl!"

'I argued, "So? None of your boys remembered the shloka! I did. Which means that my mind is capable of learning too! So tell me why I cannot join the school if I can remember everything better than the boys."

'Gangal Kaka tried to scare me by saying, "Because you will bring the curse of death on your father if you study."

'My face went pale. But in hindsight, I realize that Gangal Kaka just wanted to win the argument. So he said whatever he thought would scare me. But his terrible lie had the desired effect. I never went anywhere near the school again. If I had to make a choice between learning to read and my father's life, I would always choose my father!'

Cynthia Farrar nodded in understanding.

'But my mind wouldn't settle. Why did I have to make this choice? Why didn't the boys have to make it too, I wondered. So a few months later, I asked my father whether he would die if I studied. He laughed and dismissed my fears.

'However, he explained that our shastras forbade girls from studying, although he did not know the reason why. It was only after my marriage to Shetji that I understood—fear is the only way the Brahmins can control us. They will say anything to keep us ignorant.

'My father is hale and hearty, and I have been studying for the last seven years.'

Fatima stood up and clapped loudly for her friend.

Cynthia Farrar then introduced a young girl, Sonthi, who was sitting scared in the group. 'Sonthi is the wife of the headman of the neighbouring village. She was abused by her husband. I want you to join me in welcoming this child of God to be with us so she can earn her livelihood by helping in the kitchen and can learn with us.'

Sonthi stood up and said shyly, 'After meeting you, for the first time I feel that God is indeed merciful and that he loves us all. But is it only your God that is merciful? What about mine?'

'God is always merciful, my child. He has a very large heart and lets everyone in. We are all his children. It is the people who claim to know God personally and interpret him that create misunderstandings,' explained Farrar.

It was an emotional day, and everyone was overwhelmed. Fatima and Savitri, who shared a room, were pensive after they returned from class.

Cynthia Farrar was a devout Christian. The daughter of Phinehas, a farmer, and his wife Abigail Farrar, Cynthia had joined the congregational church in Marlborough, New Hampshire, at the young age of fifteen. She had originally come to Bombay in 1827 from Boston. She was the first unmarried woman recruited by the American Board of Commissioners for Foreign Missions (ABCFM) to oversee the development of female education. By 1829, she had set up ten vernacular free schools for girls with 400 pupils under instruction. She had to return to America briefly for health reasons. When she came back in 1839, she settled in Ahmednagar in the home of Mr and Mrs Burgess and their son Edwin.

It was not unusual for Savitri and Fatima to overhear conversations about 'the work of the Christian missionaries among heathens' and how they had no regrets about the sacrifices they had made.

'All around us we see people converting to Christianity. But we are not heathens. We have our own faith,' Fatima said to Savitri as they sat in their room.

'Yes. We do. But you and I are the luckier ones. Usman Bhai will move heaven and earth for you, and Shetji has never even raised his voice at me, let alone harass me. Sonthi, on the other hand, was harassed for no reason other than the fact that she is a woman.'

Fatima persisted with her argument, 'But what is the connection between education and faith? I can desire an education but not to convert my religion.'

Savitri laughed. 'You're right. Most people back home think that Shetji and I are going to convert. It is the most ridiculous rumour I have ever heard. But it is the only thing that the Brahmins can use to turn people against us. When we set up our schools, we will make them completely free from links to any caste or religion.'

'You are right, Aapa.[75] The Mission schools for girls are educating either Brahmins or higher-caste Hindus. Nobody is thinking about the Shudras, Mahars, Mangs and Atishudras. So many brilliant Muslim girls too have no hope. They cannot be taught by men, and so they never end up going to school. Our school must be outside of the Mission framework so we can encourage women from all castes and religions to join.'

Thus, far away from home, two young women were firming their resolve. After finishing their course, they returned to Poona. Later, in a letter to her friend Joanna Smith, dated 23 November 1848,[76] Cynthia wrote:

'In Nuggar (India) and the villages around, many are seeking to know the Lord and obey his word. Eight were received into the Church here in September.'

Girls in the school were also converting, as per this letter.

'Three girls of the boarding school have received baptism with a view of being united to the Church in the next communion. This has exerted the severest persecutions we have ever experienced. No method is left untried for breaking up all our schools. The two under my care . . . have scarcely survived the persecution of Brahmins and other influential Hindoos. But they begin to

75 Urdu word for elder sister.

76 The Grant Burr family papers published by the American Antiquarian Society in 2008.

revive and it is delightful to see the increased love which the dear girls manifest for their Christian lessons.'

Cynthia Farrar's work as a missionary was an integral part of her identity. However, she had the vision to teach girls without insisting that they convert to Christianity. In her eyes, teaching them was itself an act of service to God, even though spreading the Christian faith was one of the goals of the Mission. Farrar's contribution must not be forgotten. She created room for Fatima and Savitri and hundreds of other girls to express themselves. Perhaps the greatest gift she gave them was to allow for differences in beliefs to coexist, to be able to look beyond religion as the only force that defined relations between people. History will always be grateful to Cynthia Farrar for laying the foundation on which Savitri and Fatima became teachers.

When Farrar died in 1862, the funeral was a sight to behold. Female teachers and students of all castes and religions attended. The schools for Hindu girls that Farrar had founded in Bombay continued to be referred to as the Farrar Schools in the American Marathi Mission reports till as late as 1911.[77]

Her funeral was also the last time that Fatima and Savitri met.

77 Susan Hill Lindley and Eleanor J. Stebner, *The Westminster Handbook to Women In American Religious History*, (John Knox Press, 2005)

'The amount of entertaining accomplished in a year by a Colonel's wife in India would if set down in full, contrast curiously with the hospitality shown by a woman of the same standing in England. India is the land of dinners just as England is the land of 5 o'clock teas . . . the wives of subalterns and junior civilians—whose cheery informal little parties of six or eight are by no means to be despised by lovers of good company and simple fare . . . all of Anglo India is in the state of giving or receiving this—the most delightful or the most excruciating form of hospitality. No wonder that being a cloth merchant was a lucrative business.'

—Miss Maud Diver, *The Englishwoman in India*[78]

78 Miss Maud Diver, *The Englishwoman in India*, (W. Blackwood and Sons, 1909).

Section 7
Usman Sheikh

It was men like Usman Sheikh who contributed to changing the definition of the word 'sharif'—which used to mean grooming, etiquette, aesthetics, familiarity with Persian and Urdu, and the art of elegant conversation—such that it also came to signify social practices, which included hard work, religiosity and self-discipline.

In 1781, Warren Hastings, the first governor-general of Bengal, set up the Calcutta madrasa for the study and teaching of Muslim law and related subjects. This gave a fillip to the upward mobility of the lower classes, which had previously been excluded from higher education.

As the British became politically and administratively involved in India, the privileges that the ashraf (ruling-class) Muslims enjoyed were fast disappearing. Institutions where ashraf men exerted influence, such as the administration, courts and mosques, underwent extensive changes under the British and the authority of elite Muslim men waned. The British instituted their own legal system, leaving only family law to be regulated by Muslims. Furthermore, since religion was privatized, the ulema also began to lose their public authority.

On the other hand, the situation of the ajlaf (lower-class) Muslims started seeing a change for the better. Other than the spread of education, what really changed things for the ajlaf was the establishment of the railway system. Traders prospered. A 'new ashraf' class rose, and included scholars, landed elites, as well as enterprising traders and merchants. The nobility was increasingly viewed as irrelevant.

Usman Sheikh was part of this new elite. He was a wealthy trader who rubbed shoulders with the British. He also developed the social standing to withstand criticism from his own community for having sent Fatima off to Ahmednagar to complete her teacher-training course. What he didn't know, though, was that his own life was about to change.

23

Miss Summer Visits India

The cheery Miss Grace Summer, aptly named, had been invited by Lady Mary Falkland (whom we have met before in the story) to Bombay in the hope that she would find a civil servant groom. Lady Falkland was the wife of the governor of Bombay, Lord Falkland (1848–53).[79] Since 1830, it had been a tradition that the governor of Bombay would spend the monsoon season in Poona, which led to his entire retinue shifting base to the city from June to October every year. This added to the city's importance and sped up the establishment of residential and government facilities in the cantonment areas.

Lady Falkland was preparing to host a soirée in the residency to mark their arrival in Poona. The civil servants being courted

79 Lord Falkland was instrumental in planning and mapping the first railway line in India, the Great Indian Peninsula Railway, to connect the city to the mofussils, in 1853.

by Miss Summer were 'three-hundred-a-year-dead-or-alive[80] men and were the object of many a maiden's affection.

It so happened that one afternoon, Lady Falkland and Miss Summer were having a cup of tea. The former had a letter in her hand. Giggling, she motioned to Miss Summer, who was curious.

'Let me read out this poem to you, dear!' Lady Falkland obliged.

I do believe entirely
In civil service ranks
The best are worth a deal of tin
And none exactly blanks
But I do believe in marrying
An 'acting' man is fudge
And do not fancy anything
Below a pucca judge![81]

'That's appalling, Lady Falkland. Who could speak so crassly?'

'They all do my dear. It's part of life in India,' said Lady Falkland with some resignation. 'But I have some good news. My ayah,[82] Lachhi, assures me that she has told just the right

---

80 Widows of deceased officers were entitled to £300 a year, leading to a popular saying that an Indian Civil Service marriage was worth 'three hundred a year alive or dead', as mentioned in Philip Mason, *The Men Who Ruled India*, (Rupa Publications, 1992).

81 This is a poem written by Miss Arabella Green in the book compiled by Aliph Cheem titled *Lays of Ind—Comical, Satirical and Descriptive Poems Illustrative of English Life in India*, (Thacker Spink & Co, 1871). We are making the assumption that it was written much earlier than it was compiled.

82 British memsahibs used to keep several Indian servants which they claimed was due to the religious and social practices of the indigenous population. Because of their religious sentiments, Muslim servants

person to come home to show us some fabric and sew the perfect dress for you for the weekend soirée.'

'Oh, that won't be necessary, Lady Falkland. I have so many dresses.'

'In that case, maybe she can liven up one of your dresses with some Indian-themed finery. Our mauves and taupe won't work here; the men have gotten accustomed to seeing more colour in India.'

They were interrupted by the arrival of Fatima Sheikh. Lady Falkland and Miss Summer met her in the veranda.

Upon Lady Falkland's insistence, Miss Summer brought out a yellow gown to show Fatima.

Fatima was taken in by the colour and said admiringly, 'This yellow is rare. It is the yellow of konnappoo, a beautiful flower common in Kerala. My Malayali friend at Farrar madam's school used to wear this colour a lot. None of us had it, so we envied her. It's such a perfect yellow, neither too flashy nor too pale.'

Miss Summer was quite taken in by Fatima's gushing observations about the colour. She remarked with wonder, 'You speak English so well and express yourself so beautifully.'

'I can not only speak, but I can teach too! I am a trained teacher from Madam Mitchell and Cynthia Farrar's institution,' said Fatima with pride.

Miss Summer smiled; Fatima was a happy, disarming chatterbox if she had ever seen one. 'Can you put some flowers on the gown, perhaps around here, to enhance it?'

'Yes, yes,' agreed Fatima enthusiastically.

---

did not touch pork while Hindu servants did not touch beef. Often, both refused to serve wine and were unwilling to remove dirty dishes from the table or wash them. Ayahs were hired specifically to look after children. They were widows and would also wash dirty dishes if required.

To ensure that she had understood Miss Summer correctly, Fatima removed a few embroidered flowers from her bag and placed them on the dress. Her sense of proportion and colour were spot on.

Miss Summer was impressed. 'I must say, Lady Falkland, this is a very talented young woman. I daresay she will liven up my dress.'

Lady Falkland gave Fatima a patronizing smile and asked her to return the next day with some fabric samples and embroideries. Lachhi looked approvingly at Fatima. After all, she had vouched for her. Miss Summer also suggested that Fatima visit the library on her next visit.

As soon as she left, Lady Falkland remarked how conversations with locals must be kept brief, for fear that they may be carrying some disease!

Miss Summer did not particularly like the remark.

Carefree Fatima, with a spring in her step, started the journey back home. There was a time when Usman had not allowed her to make such visits. However, over time, she had started going to the homes of British memsahibs who loved her and that had helped Usman accept these visits. The memsahibs swore by her skills.

The minute she reached home, Fatima spotted Usman and started talking nineteen to the dozen.

'Bhaijaan, you should have seen this girl, Miss Summer. Her complexion is better than a pink rose. So beautiful! And the yellow dress; you remember I told you about Malli's konnappoo-yellow dress? Same colour. Ditto! Hai Rabba! Miss Summer is going to look like a vision in that dress.'

Usman was busy doing the accounts for the day. He did not even look up, but the corner of his mouth was curved into a smile.

Fatima continued, 'Tomorrow, I'm going to ask her for a book. An English book.'

Usman looked up, 'Why her? Go to Lizzit Sahab's library. He will give you any number of books!'

Fatima responded impatiently, 'I know that. But there's something very warm about Miss Summer. I want to become her friend.'

Usman raised his eyebrows. 'When will you stop living in a fool's paradise? The British are not our friends.'

But Fatima had vanished. She had decided to sew the flowers onto the gown herself, even though any number of the girls she had trained could have done it. After all, it had to be perfect.

Fatima had many loyal customers. Lady Maria Graham was one. She did not have any children, so she would invite Fatima for tea, and they would sit and sew together. One day Lady Graham showed Fatima how to do raised embroidery, which was three dimensional. She had learnt how to do it back in England. Fatima made her a woollen shawl as a gift. Lady Graham always introduced Fatima to women who had come to India to spend 'just a season' and who needed silks to take back as gifts.

Fatima was comfortable among British women; she could speak in English and even though the manner in which they spoke was different, she had started understanding them better after her return from Ahmednagar. Usman, for all his personal views, maintained cordial relationships with the British officers who thought of the siblings as quite helpful.

From gowns to uniforms, if they needed fabric, they would summon him.

24

Teatime

The social atmosphere in Poona was one of great contentment. All the officers were certain to get promotions regularly, there was enough prosperity for all to partake of, and the English community was large enough to have meaningful interactions. The men and women found croquet partners at the gymkhana. And if you wanted to sew, there would always be a group of women who would give you company.

The buzz that season was that such-and-such person had access to such-and-such gramophone records, and that it would no longer be necessary to find someone to sing at dinner parties. It was quite a relief, given that the singers were often not the most accomplished.

To gather meaningful information about the season ahead, Lady Falkland had invited Mrs Koofter and Mrs Hamilton, the wives of two civil service officers stationed in Poona, for tea one afternoon. She wanted, of course, to know more about suitable officers from the Green Book, which listed all the civil servants.

As Koofter and Hamilton were officers, rank demanded that their wives couldn't refuse a tea invitation from Lady Falkland. Besides, if they could help her tide over the four months from June to September, perhaps promotions might be expedited for their husbands too!

The guests arrived, bearing mangoes, which would be available for just a couple of weeks more.

'One a day is quite enough,' ventured Mrs Koofter, adding that several officers were down with 'Poonaitis'—a form of diarrhoea caused by consuming one too many of the delicious fruits. And, by Jove, were they sweet!

The ladies then made enquiries about Lady Falkland's cook. 'Have you got one of those Goans trained in Mumbai?' enquired Mrs Hamilton with a look of concern. 'They are apt to serve tomato sauce from a bottle, and they haven't the foggiest about a good roast duck with apple sauce. I taught mine painstakingly well and I'm happy to send him over if it helps.'

Lady Falkland was happy to let wives of British officers help plan her soirée, because if they could take credit for it, they would naturally declare that all of her dinners were a success.

'There's also a trader who can bring Persian fruits, pistachios, apricots and cherries from Surat,' offered Mrs Koofter, not to be outdone. 'Since we cannot serve beef or pork, it is quite convenient to have some of these things on hand to serve, or even use as stuffing.'

'Wonderful,' agreed Lady Falkland.

They then moved on to discuss the mosquito menace in Poona.

Lady Falkland exclaimed, 'It could not be worse than the prickly heat I have just come from in Bombay.'

Miss Summer recalled she had read something to the effect of:

Every nincompoop you meet
Has a cure for prickly heat.
I'll tell you for a song,
That all of them are wrong.

Agreeable laughter followed, and Mrs Hamilton and Mrs Koofter declared that the Goan cook had outdone himself. He certainly knew how to make cakes—they were just the right flavour and texture to go with the tea.

Miss Summer enquired, 'Do you know Fatima?'

Mrs Hamilton was quite lavish in her praise. 'The girl is very skilful. In fact, her brother Usman is particularly resourceful with fabrics. If not for him, Poona might be insufferable. It might be worth paying his shop a visit,' she suggested.

'And word is that he has remained unmarried to protect his sister,' Mrs Koofter added, quickly restoring the balance of information provided in her favour. 'Which is also quite nice, because he's attractive in his own way. Our adventurous Mrs Butler made frequent trips to his shop, we hear, but to no avail.'

Lady Falkland wondered why this piece of information mattered, given that she was nudging them to suggest eligible civil servants for Miss Summer. But perhaps due to rank or other reasons, neither Mrs Koofter nor Mrs Hamilton suggested a single eligible civil servant.

The conversation moved on to servants—their cleanliness and their propensity for small lies and petty thefts; one sent them to buy something and they always added a small commission to it. But, the ladies acknowledged, they never asked for an evening off and were very reliable. The ayahs were particularly good, and if they were widows, exceedingly honest.

And thus having suitably agreed on everything, the ladies took their leave. Lady Falkland considered the evening quite futile. Miss Summer, however, was now determined to visit Usman's shop.

25

Fatima Makes a Friend

True to her word, Fatima took the embroidered dress back to Lady Falkland's house the next day. As she entered, Mrs Koofter and Mrs Hamilton were leaving the house after tea and exchanged pleasantries with her.

Fatima was shown to the veranda, where Miss Summer was eagerly awaiting her. Fatima unwrapped the gown for her to see.

Miss Summer exclaimed, 'This is delightful, what you've done with it.'

Fatima nodded and smiled. 'Thank you.'

Lady Falkland butted in, 'And what do you have for me today?'

Fatima laid out several fabric samples and embroidery patches for them to see. She had exceeded herself. There were greens paired with purple, mauve paired with orange and even a peacock blue paired with a chocolate brown that was most delightful. Finally, Mrs Falkland opted for a mauve-and-orange gown with fine silk embroidery.

Miss Summer, however, hadn't chosen anything. She asked Fatima, 'Do you have a shop where I can come and see more fabrics?'

Lady Falkland was able to connect the desire to visit the fabric shop to the teatime conversation the previous evening and did not object. Ayah Lacchi offered to take Miss Summer to Usman's cloth shop.

The next morning, Miss Summer's carriage pulled up in front of Usman's textile shop. Miss Summer was as beautiful as Fatima had described, and despite his own sense of caution, Usman found himself admiring her.

'Welcome, Miss Summer. My sister Fatima had mentioned that you would be coming to our shop.'

Miss Summer also took a good look at Usman before enquiring, 'Isn't she here?'

'No, she's a bit under the weather. She has been straining herself a lot, and it's taken a toll on her,' responded Usman.

'It's so wonderful that both you and Fatima speak English so well.'

'It's part and parcel of the world we live in. What may I show you?' asked Usman, quick to do some business.

'Anything that you believe will look good on me. But only if you call me by my Christian name, Grace.'

So Grace and Usman spent the afternoon admiring fabrics. Grace did brush her fingers across Usman's on more than one occasion as she pretended to peruse the fabrics intently. Muhasibji smiled in complicit approval. Fatima had blurted out all kinds of favourable things about Miss Summer to him as well.

Usman, who had lived an ascetic life for the sake of his sister, was not immune to her charms, even though Grace's moves were innocent. The art of seduction wasn't something she had yet learnt.

As she was about to leave, she said, 'Usman, I have never had such a lovely afternoon. I hope I will see you again!'

'Yes. Have you chosen anything so Fatima may bring it to you?'

'Yes, I like your lemon-green silk fabric with baby-pink embroidery, and I should very much like a gown made from that. Fatima has my measurements,' she added suggestively.

Usman smiled as Grace took her leave.

Grace found herself wondering whether she would have to choose someone from among the pitiable pool of civil servants. Couldn't a man who had set up a flourishing textile business fit the bill? And then she laughed at how preposterous it all sounded.

The next day, of course, Muhasibji gave Fatima an elaborate account of the chemistry between Usman and Grace Summer. Fatima had found someone she could tease her brother about, even though they all thought that nothing much would come of it.

Section 8

The First School, 1848

As evidenced in the preceding chapters, after Fatima and Savitri returned from Ahmednagar, Fatima got busy with her brother's business, with the promise that as soon as Savitri needed her to work in any matter relating to education, she would make herself available.

In the meantime, Jyoti and Savitri were trying to arrange a place and some funds to start a school for girls.

26

The School in Bhidewada

In 1846, Sagunabai Kshirsagar had tried to start a school in Maharwada for the Shudras. Several Ponga Pandits came together to shut it down.

'Saguna is a widow who has lost her mind! She has lived with Father John and his family for far too long and now she wants to change the religion of the Mahars,' was a criticism she often heard. But this was a common allegation hurled at all social reformers of the time.

One day, Savitri asked Sagunabai, 'These Prabhus who were against your work, what was the worst thing they ever said to you?'

'Savitri, if there is one thing my own life has taught me, it is to forget the past. You are a strong woman, so keep an eye on the future. Steel yourself! You will be called unspeakable words that you haven't heard before. The Prabhus will stop at nothing to destroy your identity and your reputation.'

Savitri understood Sagunabai's concern. However, she and Jyoti were determined to push forward. Hence, on Christmas day in 1846, a big congregation of Shudras and Atishudras was called. Jyotirao spoke to the crowd and explained to them that they should understand who the real enemy is.

'What Brahmins teach and what Hinduism is all about are two different things. They are scared that if the Mahars and other Shudras get educated, they cannot be ruled through fear. The Brahmins quote the so-called scriptures, but they don't let us get educated. If you don't listen to Brahmins, you will be born as a rat in the next life, they say. Where is the proof of this?'

Tatya Saheb Bhide, a Brahmin by birth and lawyer in the employ of Maharaja Scindia[83] of Gwalior, who owned a house in Poona called Bhidewada, was listening intently.

Jyotirao announced at the sabha that he would start a school for girls. 'Our girls cannot go to Brahmin schools. Brahmins, teachers, won't come to where we live. Are we to remain ignorant all our lives?' he demanded.

Tatya Saheb Bhide was energized by Jyoti's speech. He agreed to give space in his house for the school. Within a year, Jyoti, Savitri and his friends Sakharam and Keshav created a basic framework for the school. Savitri was appointed teacher and headmistress and Fatima was also appointed as a teacher. The school opened on 1 January 1848.

Some historians suggest that both the Hindu and the Muslim community opposed Fatima for what she was doing. However, Fatima was no stranger to unforeseen tragedies in her life. When she had accompanied Savitri, hand-in-hand, on their journey to gain legitimacy as teachers, the events that played out made both

83 As reported in Dhananjay Keer's biography *Mahatma Jyotirao Phuley*, (Popular Prakashan, 2012).

of them develop skins as thick as that of a hippopotamus (and that's putting it mildly).

On the early morning of 3 January, as Fatima was walking from her home to the school in Bhidewada, a heap of cow dung hit her smack in the face! The stench was unbearable.

Fatima ran to the school and went straight to the bathroom. With a small piece of soap, she scrubbed her face till the smell of dung was washed away. Then she came out of the bathroom, sat outside the door, put her face in her hands and stared into the open space in front. She was shivering, but not with fear; she was upset that she had let the act affect her.

Fatima always hid her tiredness behind her cheerful nature and humour; but today, she let herself feel the exhaustion. The evening before she had received a jolt. Ribbi, a girl who lived in the neighbourhood, all of nine years old, was going to be married off to a forty-year-old widower! Had she spent too much time with British memsahibs, helping them with their clothes? Had she lost touch with her own people? All Fatima could see in front of her eyes was Ribbi.

Just then, Savitri entered.

Fatima told Savitri what had happened the previous day. She was trembling. 'How can Ribbi's nikah be arranged with a forty-year-old man!'

Savitri hugged her tight. 'Don't lose heart,' she said.

'How are we ever going to change anything? I cannot take Ribbi from her house and bring her here. Her father won't let me.' Fatima was despondent.

'Fatima, I have no idea what to do, but we have to take it one step at a time. We enrolled six girls yesterday—that is a start. And maybe we cannot save everyone.'

Savitri picked up the enrolment register lying nearby and read out loud, 'Annapurna Jogi, Sumite Mokashi, Durga Deshmukh,

Madhavi Dhanna, Sonu Pawar and Arna Kardle. Maybe we can change their lives to begin with!'

Fatima continued, 'Ribbi is very bright. Do you remember the bed sheet that she embroidered for me? Such intricate, progressive patterns! There is so much mathematics in everything she does.'

Savitri nodded in understanding.

'Salim, Ribbi's father, screamed at me, saying, "Why do girls need to learn anything except how to keep the house? I don't want my daughter to end up unmarried like you!"'

Savitri knew that many Muslims saw Fatima as someone who was 'un-anchored' and 'free'. She decided to lighten the mood.

'Maybe you should make Salim meet Limaye,' she suggested. 'Today, on the road, he stopped me and told me that if an educated girl cooks, the food becomes poison.'

'Then first let us educate Limaye's wife and see the result!'

The idea was so hare-brained that both Fatima and Savitri burst out laughing. For a moment, Fatima didn't know whether she was laughing or crying. Small joys on an otherwise difficult day.

Fatima looked at Savitri in admiration as she asked, 'Aapa, don't you ever get angry?'

'Fatima, it is best that you don't know about my temper! Once, when I was small, I saw a snake going up a tree to eat eggs from a nest. I pelted it with so many stones that the poor thing ran away. Sometimes I wonder, what if the snake had attacked me? What would I have done? I have always been foolish and short-tempered. But with Shetji, I have become mature,' conceded Savitri.

'But you saved those eggs,' Fatima reminded her.

'But for how long? I couldn't have prevented another snake from coming five minutes later. Unless the birds learn to fly, I cannot help. It is in the snake's nature to eat eggs.'

Fatima listened keenly. Savitri, it seemed, was no longer talking about snakes but rather about human behaviour.

'Similarly, unless we can educate more Salims and Ribbis, we cannot always be there to prevent mishaps.'

Fatima nodded, 'Aapa, it is unfortunate that the birth of a girl has always been unwelcome. Do you know that Amir Khusrau, the scholar, mourned the birth of his daughter—"I wish you were not born and if you were, it would have been better if you had been a boy".'[84]

'In our rituals too, there is a blessing, "putravati bhava", which means may you beget a son. The fact remains that if nobody begets daughters, there will be no sons,' said Savitri.

Fatima sighed. 'Our fight is that of a hundred years or more.'

The two of them got back to work. Savitri made a poster saying '*Sakshar Vha, Nirbhar Vha*'—Become Literate and Become Independent.

She hung it outside the school.

In the days that followed, Savitri started carrying an extra saree with her because she was regularly pelted with stones and filth. The Brahmins realized that she was not afraid of them. And that made them very afraid!

---

84 Hajira Kumar, *Status of Muslim Women in India,* (Aakar Books, 2002).

27
Homeless

The Brahmins were livid with Jyotirao.

Initially, he was educating his own wife. They had taken him to the Peshwa's darbar to no avail. Then, he had joined forces with Usman and Fatima Sheikh. Now he had started a school to teach girls of backward castes in Bhidewada. This school had grown to having nine girls, which was not much. But now they heard that he was scouting for a place to open another school for Mahars and Mangs. This was nothing short of sacrilege, and he had to be stopped!

Purohitji, Maha Pandit Bhattji and a host of Brahmins gathered at Govindrao's house.

Purohitji threatened Govindrao, 'Generations of your family will rot in hell. What blasphemous work is Jyoti doing? Which shastras allow the education of girls and the lower castes?'

Maha Pandit Bhattji chimed in too, 'Do you know, Govindrao, that Haripant and Narayan, two brothers who taught at the

American Marathi Mission in Ahmednagar, where Savitri went to study, have converted to Christianity? They were not Mahars but Brahmins who converted.[85] Interacting with these missionaries will be the end of our religion.'

Govindrao was too timid to stand up to such an onslaught. He said, 'Why are you telling me this? You all know that since childhood Jyotirao has been an outlier. His questions, his desire to learn, everything has always been as much of a problem for me as it is for you. He does not listen to me.'

Bhatt was enraged. 'Then it is now time to remove this problem from your house, Govindrao. By keeping him in your house, you are going to bring untold misery upon yourself. Not a single flower will bloom in your plantations anymore. You will never be able to make an offering to God again. You're not welcome for worship in any temple, and we will declare you a nastik, a man of no faith.'

Purohitji continued the barrage, 'Neither you nor anyone in your family will experience punarjanam.[86] You have given birth to your own enemy in your own household. Jyotirao took away your beloved wife Chimnabai soon after his birth. Do you think he will spare you? You will rot in hell because that is where your son's deeds will send you if you do not break all ties with him immediately.'

Govindrao could no longer take this onslaught. His spirit was broken. He did not know what was right and what was wrong anymore. Neither did he know if what the Brahmins were saying was true or not.

---

85 Rev. R.G. Wilder, *Mission Schools in India of the American Board of Commissioners for Foreign Missions* (ADF Randolph, 1861).

86 According to Hindu belief, all beings go through birth, life, death and rebirth (punarjanam), and this is known as the cycle of samsara.

With a heavy heart, he asked Jyoti and his wife Savitri to leave his home. This was in 1849. Both Jyoti and Savitri understood Govindrao's plight and did not hate him for it. This made it even more difficult for Govindrao.

'Do not worry, Baba,' said Jyotirao. 'If people come to trouble you, tell them that Jyoti does not live here any more. If they wish to talk to me or change my mind about opening the school in Bhidewada, they are free to meet me.'

Govindrao was distraught with guilt. He looked at Jyoti and pleaded, 'Why are you behaving this way? Do you have no attachment to me? Did I raise you, educate you, so that one day your work takes you away from me?'

'Baba, please do not think that way. Our relationship is too strong to be broken.'

'Your poor wife Savitri is being insulted daily. People spit on her, threaten to violate her and pelt her with cow dung and stones. Are you all right with that?' asked Govindrao.

'Balwantrao Sakharamji Kolhe and the village Pattewala walk with her every day for her safety. And she knows that only cowards throw cow dung,' Jyoti tried to allay Govindrao's fears gently.

'I am not as strong as you are, Jyoti. I do not have the strength to fight all these people.' Govindrao felt ashamed of his predicament.

'Baba, for generations on end, we have been taught to keep our head hanging low and bear all insults without retaliation. So, I understand that you're afraid. But I have chosen my path. With great difficulty, many people have joined me, making the Brahmins their enemy in the process. If I stop, their spirits will be crushed.'

Saying this, Jyotirao looked at Savitri expectantly. She expressed her agreement with her eyes and went and touched Govindrao's feet.

Govindrao wondered where Jyoti would go with his young wife. The thought made him sick with pain. Sagunabai was a silent spectator to this conversation. Not because she couldn't say much, but because she didn't want to. She could see that the paths of the father and son were diverging, and perhaps that was for the best for both.

Jyoti and Savitri went to pack their belongings. They put all their books and possessions in a big bag and paid their respects to Govindrao and Sagunabai before leaving.

The minute they left their home, they knew they could not look back lest Govindrao's remorse stop them. As the wind made friends with their tears, they kept walking, without a clue as to where to go or what to do for the night.

It seems that their feet knew something they didn't.

They found themselves outside Munshi Gafar Baig's house.

28

Welcome Home

Gafar Baig was not surprised at the way things had turned out for Jyoti and Savitri.

'Baig Sahab, I never expected that the Brahmins would brainwash my father to this extent. I do not feel bad for myself in the least, but for my beautiful wife, who is homeless tonight,' confessed Jyotirao.

Baig Sahab said gently, 'Govind has always been a little weak-willed when it comes to standing up to the pressure of these people. He will come to his senses. Meanwhile, Savitri is my daughter so she will never be homeless. Let me first organize a place to stay for you.'

A realization suddenly hit Jyoti and he said, 'My wife walked out with me without questioning my decision. I don't know if I can ever repay her.'

'She is the wind beneath your wings, Jyoti. Never forget that.'

As tea was served, Baig Sahab wrote a letter to Usman Sheikh, which he then dispatched through his manservant. In the letter, he asked Usman and Fatima to offer the Phule couple food, shelter and unconditional support for a few months.

The Sheikh siblings lived in a reasonably large house. And Usman never said no to his beloved Baig Chacha, who was a father figure to him. So, he wrote back in the affirmative and asked Fatima to ready a room immediately. Fatima couldn't believe her ears—was this really happening? What could be better than to live with Savitri, her companion and friend?

It was a solemn moment when Savitri entered Fatima's home. As Fatima welcomed her with a hug, Usman opened his arms to Jyoti. Khadija Bi, who lived with Usman and Savitri, laid out dinner. There wasn't much conversation during dinner, just an unspoken sense of mutual regard. Fatima, who couldn't contain her excitement, finally broke the silence and said, 'Aapa, Bhaijaan, our Mohammed Paighambar has said, "*Tum dharti waalon par daya karo, aakashwala (Allah) tum par daya karega.*" Consider this your own house and don't worry about anything. Allah will show the way.'

It took a couple of days for Jyoti to realize that leaving home was a blessing. Now that Govindrao was spared the trouble of having to constantly explain his son's actions, Jyoti felt liberated.

A few years ago, Jyoti had been insulted and thrown out of a Brahmin friend's wedding procession, which was when he had realized that societal norms were warped. Change was long overdue. With a wife like Savitri he had the courage to not merely consider the idea of women's liberation and social upliftment, but to truly commit to it. Jyoti also believed that women could overcome their oppression only through their own will, efforts and autonomy.[87] Savitri and Fatima were both exemplar women in that sense.

As the couple settled into their new home, Saguna Aau often came to visit them, bringing food or grains. She always made it a point to mention that Govindrao was extremely concerned about their welfare and kept asking about them.

Savitri had a practical head on her shoulders. Despite their warm welcome at the Sheikhs' house, she knew two things—one, they would have to find a way to seek Govindrao's forgiveness and convince him to take them back, and second, that Jyoti and she had to find a source of income if they wished to sustain their work.

For a while, they continued the school in Bhidewada. However, as the girls were the children of Mahars and Mangs, they were not allowed to drink water from the nearby water sources. Fatima and Savitri could not bear to see the children go thirsty. So, they had to start purchasing water for the children. The funds they were getting were not enough to run the school on a sustained basis. Hence, the Bhidewada school was closed for a brief time.

The Brahmins rejoiced. Some even went to celebrate in the Bavan Khani, the house of fifty-two rooms that was set up around 1748, during the reign of Balaji Baji Rao. It was a place that the Peshwas and Brahmins would visit for pleasure. By the nineteenth century, the Bavan Khani had a notorious reputation, and it had taken prostitution to locals. There, the Brahmins had a rousing celebration of the failure of the Bhidewada school. But their revelry was short-lived.

Savitri had resolved that she would come back stronger.

---

87 This thought echoed those of John Stuart Mill and Friedrich Engels. Jyotirao Phule believed that women had a crucial role in bringing about social change, and the development of their rational faculties via education was significant.

29

Rebuilding the Schools

At Usman and Fatima's place, there was a plethora of scrap cloth. So Savitri started stitching blankets with this cloth to supplement their income. Both Jyoti and Savitri worked tirelessly to earn a living. One afternoon, Savitri was tending to a bag of leftover cloth pieces, segregating the usable from the unusable ones. Then, she arranged all the usable pieces in a square in front of her and gestured to Jyoti, who was sitting before her with a book, to help her. 'Shetji, please take the needle and thread and help me sew this blanket.'

The two of them took up opposite ends and worked quietly, deep in thought.

Finally, Savitri said, 'Shutting Bhidewada seems like we have admitted defeat.'

Jyoti nodded. 'I heard that the Brahmins celebrated our failure. We don't have any female teachers other than you and

Fatima. The objections to sending the girls to school will be easier to manage if we have female teachers.'

Savitri had an idea. 'Why don't you ask Bhawalkar, Paranjpe and Govande to start teaching their wives? Govande's wife Saraswati[88] seems to be the most enthusiastic about education.'

'Bhawalkar was suggesting the same thing,' said Jyoti. 'It aligns with the work that Dadoba Pandurang[89] wants to do at the Paramahansa Sabha[90] in Pune. Walvekar is also ready to help.'

'That's great! We also need to factor in funds for both food and water. I believe that if we can lure the girls in with a free meal, we can send them back with an education,' said the visionary young wife.

Jyoti nodded and smiled. 'And we thought that all we needed was a blackboard and chalk to start a school! By the way, have you seen Usman and Fatima at work? This brother-and-sister jodi are even more forward-thinking than we are, Savitri. They have money and they have the networks. Though I feel that since they're already giving us shelter, we must not ask them for anything else.'

Savitri nodded in agreement and added, 'Whenever I tell Fatima I want something, she gets it done. The other day, I wanted to make some new language worksheets for the students.

---

88 Saraswati Govande was also very active in the schools run by the Phules.

89 Dadoba Pandurang (Tarkhadkar) (1814–1882) was a renowned social reformer, writer, and linguist from Bombay.

90 Kenneth W. Jones and Gordon Johnson, *Socio-religious Reform Movements in British India,* (Cambridge University Press, 1989). The Paramahansa Sabha was primarily interested in breaking caste rules. At their meetings, members ate food cooked by lower-caste people. They also advocated women's education and widow remarriage.

She designed them overnight and brought them to the school the next morning. It is clear that she values this work so much that she cannot bear to see anything left undone.'

Thus, the process of reform was reinitiated. Saraswati Govande and a few other wives were trained to become proper teachers. Soon, a school for girls was opened in Peth Joon Ganj at a place provided by Sadashiv Govande, as no one else was willing to offer their properties. Govande also provided slates and Rs 2 per month for distributing food to the children. The principal of Poona College, Major Thomas Candy, sent a stack of books as a contribution from his side.

Jyoti was elated that they had been able to open another school. He proceeded to travel to nearby areas such as Meethganj, Bhavani Peth and Nana Peth and talked extensively with the people. He exhorted them to start sending their children to schools where they would get food for the mind and food for the tummy.

The Brahmins planned to shut down this school as well. The difference was that this time, in their attacks against the couple, they chose a surrogate victim, a bright young girl named Kashi, the daughter of Dr Vishram Ramji Ghollay.

Dr Ghollay had just returned home from his rounds when someone knocked at the door. It was Purohitji. Kashi, his daughter, ran to open the door.

Purohit dismissed the girl. 'Ae ladki, move away. Otherwise I will curse you to be reborn as a lizard!'

Kashi said playfully, 'And I will curse you to be reborn as a fly!'

She then started laughing.

Ghollay heard what was happening and came out to see Purohitji fuming with rage and Kashi running around the house, clapping, leaping and singing.

Ghollay reluctantly said, 'Purohitji, do come inside.'

Purohitji admonished him, 'I have not come here to be insulted by your chit of a daughter. I have told you not to send her to school. Have you no fear of God? Do you know what curses can befall your family if you educate your daughter?'

Ghollay was tired of this. 'Purohitji, I don't believe in these curses. I'm a doctor. I can say with certainty that a Brahmin's body is no different from a Shudra's body or a Mahar's body. Maybe you should also start to think this way.'

'Think which way? Is it all right for your daughter to insult me? One day, she will feel she is superior to her husband and run away from him. Worse, her husband will be poisoned by the water she gives him to drink, and she will become a widow at an early age,' he ranted.

'Please show me the shastra where this is written, Purohitji,' asked Ghollay.

'Oh! So you want to show me that you can read for yourself! Don't be surprised when the wrath of God wreaks havoc in your household,' cursed Purohitji.

Ghollay did not believe a word Purohitji was saying.

Ghollay added, 'Jyoti bhau[91] and Savitri vahini[92] are doing what Krishna bhagwan himself has said in the Bhagwad Geeta, "The wise work for the welfare of the world."'

Purohitji left in a huff. Ghollay was exhausted from his day and this exchange. So he had dinner and retired.

Purohitji wanted to make an example of Ghollay. He had his cronies bribe one of Ghollay's relatives to poison Kashi.[93] They

---

91 Bhau is a Marathi word that means brother.

92 Vahini is a Marathi word that means sister-in-law.

93 R. Goswami, 'Know your city: Savitribai Phule and the first modern school for girls she opened in Pune,' *The Indian Express*, 26 February 2022.

wanted to spread the fear that girls who learnt how to read and write would die an untimely death.[94]

Ghollay woefully realized that the 'wrath of God' was just the jealousy of the Brahmins. He took his daughter's body to Purohitji's house along with the man bribed to poison Kashi and said, 'When you threatened me first, I had something to lose. Now I have lost Kashi, so I have nothing to lose or fear. The consequences of disobeying you have nothing to do with disobeying God. Because God does not kill people. Upon my daughter's body, it is my turn to curse you now! The days of your blind rule are numbered. I will dedicate myself to the awakening that has been started by Jyoti bhau and Savitri vahini.'

Ghollay was an iron-willed man.

Despite his loss, he had his second daughter Gangu educated as well.[95] Such was the incredible energy of social change seeded at the time.

---

94 R. Goswami, 'Know your city: Savitribai Phule and the first modern school for girls she opened in Pune,' *The Indian Express*, 26 February 2022.

95 Shraddha Kumbhojkar, Head of the History Department, Savitribai Phule Pune University, narrates this story in the above article in *The Indian Express* by R. Goswami.

Section 9

Consolidating the Work

During the period from 1848 to 1853, Jyoti, Savitri and their friends opened eighteen schools.[96] Not all of them survived, but they were opened with the best of intentions. Some, like Bhidewada, were shut and reopened. Sakharam and Walvekar started managing the Bhidewada school.[97] Savitri and Fatima planned the lessons delivered at their school with great care and a scientific, logical approach. Saraswati Govande stepped up to train herself to become a teacher.

---

96 See Annexure 4 for a list of schools opened by Jyotirao and Savitri Phule, Fatima Sheikh and their associates.

97 Dr Ravindra Thakur (translated from Marathi to English by Reshma Kulkarni-Pathare), *Mahatma Jyotirao Phule*, (Mehta Publishing House, 2020).

'Liberty, when it begins to take root, is a plant of rapid growth.'

—George Washington

30

Expansion of Schools (1848–1853)

The curriculum at the schools run by Jyotirao and Savitri was different from that of the schools run by the Brahmins. It covered a broad range of subjects, including the history of the Marathas, the geography of India and Asia, grammar, arithmetic and basic writings on socioeconomic problems.[98] The lower castes in particular were also taught to read the Marathi textbooks used in the government vernacular schools, such as *Niteebodhkutha* (moral stories) and the primer *Lipidara*. The curriculum was based on human development rather than on gender-specific topics.

To get more and more girls to enrol in the schools, Jyoti enlisted the help of Lahuji Ustad, who ran the local akhada

98 The list of readings given in the report of the second annual examination also contains books such as G.N. Shenvi's *Rinunishedhuk* (the evils of debt) of the Bombay Deccan Vernacular Society.

where Jyoti himself had trained. Lahuji had a tough manner of speaking, and all the locals looked up to him. So, with his encouragement, more and more people started sending their girls to school. Lahuji hated the British, but his hatred for servitude of any kind was far greater. That was why he agreed to help Jyoti recruit students.

With increasing enrolments, funds became a perennial problem that Jyoti knew he needed to solve. 'We need donations,' he confessed to Govande. 'This morning, Savitri was asking me about the Dakshina Fund, which the British revived[99] in 1821. Why don't we apply for it?'

Govande was impressed with this new idea to raise funds. Slowly but surely, the number of students who enrolled increased. Another school was opened at Anna Chiplunkar's[100] mansion at Budhwar Peth, on 3 July 1851.[101] On the first day of this school, merely eight girls were on the rolls; soon their numbers rose to

---

99 It had been a long-standing tradition under Peshwa rule that Brahmin scholars could present themselves annually to receive dakshina from the court. The colonial government had initially discontinued this practice but later resumed it, in a reduced form, to prevent large-scale protest. This was because the Chitpawan Brahmins had continued to dominate public discourse in Poona as well as in Bombay in the eighteenth century thanks to their unique position in the Peshwa administration.

In 1849, Jyotirao Phule drafted a petition to broaden the scope of the Dakshina Fund. The move caused so much opposition that the petition was never formally submitted to the government. But it was publicized widely in *Dnyanodaya* (rise of knowledge), a bilingual Anglo–Marathi periodical published by the American Marathi Mission, and the suggestions were taken up by the government of the Bombay Presidency.

100 Annasaheb Vasudev Chipunkar was a wealthy man and a progressive Brahmin.

101 Suraj Yengde, *Caste Matters*, (Penguin Random House, 2019).

forty-eight. Savitri now had a few more teachers ready, and hence she could manage more schools. By now, the hazards of walking to school had reduced; instead, people started to recognize her, and both she and Fatima earned respect for their work. By the end of 1851, over 150 girls had enrolled in the schools. This was no mean feat!

Jyoti also taught for four hours daily. He also undertook contracts on the side so he could earn an income to keep the schools going. Meanwhile, Savitri was acutely aware that Jyoti was trying to accomplish a hundred things. His vision was not limited to teaching at the schools alone. He wanted to open many other institutions and focus on learning further, writing more and sharing his ideas with as many people as possible.

Soon, Jyoti set up an acting committee and handed over the management of their schools to it[102] while seeking out more and more locations for schools himself. Sudamji Alhaat from Vetal Peth, for instance, was impressed by Jyoti and Savitri's reform work and committed space in his mansion to them. But the Brahmins threatened to ostracize him from the community, following which he withdrew his support.

Savitri and Fatima stepped up to run the schools. They spent their time visiting multiple schools in a day and teaching and administering as required. Despite the struggles, what kept the schools going was the support from the British. The schools that Fatima, Savitri, Jyoti and their associates set up between 1851 and 1853 for girls and untouchable students became beneficiaries of the Dakshina Fund via an additional grant of Rs 75 a month

102 The committee comprised Keshav Shivram Bhawalkar, Anna Sahastrabuddhe, Bapuraoji Mande, Vishnu Bhide, Krishnashastri Chiplunkar and Vishnushastri Pandit. Pandit was later known for his widow remarriage initiatives as well.

from the Dakshina Prize Fund Committee.[103] This was a major change from the original aim of the fund, which was to encourage and reward those who had become learned in the Hindu sacred books.

In 1852, the education department of the British government publicly examined the schools set up by Jyoti, Savitri and their associates. Their report states: 'The prejudice against teaching girls to read and write began to give way . . . the good conduct and honesty of the peons in conveying the girls to and from school and parental treatment and indulgent attention of the teachers made the girls love the schools and literally run to them with alacrity and joy.'

Major Thomas Candy, the principal of Poona College, also recorded in his journal that the girls studying in the three schools were intelligent and quick-witted. In November 1852, the education department felicitated the couple. In a public ceremony presided over by Major Candy, a presentation of shawls was to be made.

However, the Brahmins objected and maintained that a man of Jyoti's caste and rank should receive the lower reward of money, which was welcome to Jyoti, who was a practical man.

103 This support was thanks to a public examination in 1852, which went very well. The report said that the progress exhibited by the girls was far greater than that of any boys' schools during the period.

31

Multiple Waves of Reform

With the Dakshina Fund under threat, Maha Pandit Bhattji and other Brahmins became truly uncomfortable. They could see the writing on the wall.

Bhattji appraised the situation. 'Purohitji, we have not one enemy in Jyoti and his friends, but three enemies. First is the British legal system, which passes foolish legislations like the abolition of Sati, second is Western education and the third is the Christian missionaries. These three enemies are making life difficult for us.'

Purohitji was pensive as well. 'We have tried everything, haven't we? My father used to tell me about the time when 40,000 Brahmins would be fed the choicest of meals for days together thanks to the Dakshina Fund,' he said, his mouth watering.

Bhattji added, '*Annadanam samam danam, trilokeshu na vidhathe* (The donation of food is supreme and incomparable to any charity). This is what the shastras say. If our customs and traditions are going to break down like this, then how are we Prabhus and Brahmins to sustain ourselves? We have always enjoyed the patronage of the kings. We were the mainstay of Akbar's navratnas and the counsel in Tipu Sultan's courts. Even Aurangzeb maintained a high number of Brahmins in his darbar. The Peshwa would not take a single decision without consulting us. We have always been able to get along with all kinds of rulers. But these British don't seem to like us. They don't value our learning.'

'You are right,' agreed Purohitji. 'We should have stopped the publication of that incendiary newspaper *Prabhakar*.[104] Every Sunday, Bhau Mahajan creates more trouble. He has played havoc with people's minds by questioning the idea of Kaliyuga and laughing at our jyotish shastra. Nobody wants to believe our predictions about rainfall, times of prosperity and times of difficulty or anything else.'

Bhattji nodded and said, 'Hmmm. If Mahajan had stuck to his idea of deshkalyan to attack the British, it might have been good for all of us. But he's questioning the need for hereditary professions and is appealing to people to develop a rational and scientific view of life. The other day, Mahajan criticized a babu in Calcutta for spending Rs 13 lakh on his mother's shraadh and suggested that there were better uses for the money. After this article, many households are now spending less on the shraadh ceremony.'

'Bhau Mahajan is a pest. Do you know he wrote that for the good of Hindu society, the marriageable age for girls and

104 Bhau Mahajan was the first Maharashtrian intellectual to start an exclusively Marathi newspaper, *Prabhakar*, in 1841, and make journalism his full-time occupation. He sought out issues of injustice and exposed the evils that beset society. He was staunchly anti-British.

boys should be fixed at sixteen and twenty-one respectively?' thundered Purohitji, as if Mahajan had committed blasphemy.

Bhattji was hitting his head hard with his palms, hoping for a solution.

'Shall we appeal to the Education Commission to not give away our Dakshina Fund[105] to these Shudras?' suggested Purohitji.

Bhattji nodded and asked Purohitji to write a letter. Yet neither of them seemed confident that they would be able to pull this off.

Both wondered if they had forgotten to take into account a fourth enemy—the biggest one. The common people who were slowly escaping from the deadly noose of cause-and-effect that the Brahmins had used to rule over them for so many years. With his shoulders slouched and pride wounded, Purohitji slowly walked back home.

105 Even though in 1855 one of Jyoti's proposals to the Dakshina Fund was rejected, he continued to receive other forms of support from the government and well-wishers.

32

Individuals Contribute

Major Thomas Candy was an important well-wisher of the revolution that was underway. He wanted more people to help, and so he organized a visit by Erskine Perry,[106] the chief justice of the Bombay High Court, to the schools run by Savitri and Fatima in Poona. There is also a reference that Mr Lumsdain, the then secretary to government, accompanied Erskine Perry on this visit.[107]

When Perry met Fatima, he was deeply moved by her struggle. He knew that schools for Muslim girls were few and far between, and seeing Fatima, he felt a sense of hope. Perry was deeply influenced by both Dadabhai Naoroji's work in Bombay and Jyoti's work in Poona. Even though there is no recorded

106 Thomas Erskine Perry was the son of the radical journalist James Perry. He became a judge of the Supreme Court of Bombay in 1840, and later chief justice in 1847. He retired in 1852 and continued to publish legal works and books on Indian subjects.

107 Refer to Annexure 6 for a detailed account of this reference.

evidence that Naoroji and Jyoti ever met, Erskine Perry knew both of them well.[108]

After having gone around the classrooms, Perry sat down in one of the classrooms and remarked, 'Jyoti, like you, there is another Parsi friend of mine who is laying the groundwork for female education. His name is Dadabhai Naoroji. Unlike you, he has strong ties to prominent Shetia philanthropists such as the Camas.'

Fatima chimed in, 'I have heard of Naoroji. I heard an anecdote about him from our dear friend Miss Grace Summer who lives with Lady Falkland in Bombay. They had some Parsi guests who knew this story. Shall I tell you all?'

'Yes Fatima, please enlighten us,' encouraged Savitri.

'One day, Naoroji put his thoughts on girls' education on paper and wrote to Sir Jamsetjee Jeejeebhoy[109]—who, as you all know, is a very successful merchant and philanthropist—requesting an interview. Naoroji received a prompt answer from the generous baronet and a meeting was set at the office of the Parsi Panchayat, a guild that looked after the economic interests of the Parsi community. Jamsetjee also asked a conservative Parsi, Dossabhoy Sorabjee Munshi, to be present at the interview. At the meeting, Jamsetjee asked Naoroji to speak openly about the proposal he had in mind.

'Naoroji spoke about his intention to include girls into the ambit of education. After listening to him, Jamsetjee turned to Mr Dossabhoy saying, "Well, Munshi Sahab, what do you say to that?"

'The Munshi sahab, of course, did not approve of the novel idea of educating females. He said, "The young man wants to educate

---

108 Dinyar Phiroze Patel, 'The Grand Old Man: Dadabhai Naoroji and the Evolution of the Demand for Indian Self-Government', Doctoral dissertation, Graduate School of Arts & Sciences, Harvard University, 2015.

109 Sir Jamsetjee Jejeebhoy, first Baronet Jejeebhoy of Bombay, was an Indian-Parsi merchant and philanthropist. He made a huge fortune in cotton and the opium trade with China.

females. But what do females want education for? It will only spoil them. You see, you should not supply more oil to a lamp than it can bear, for otherwise the light is sure to extinguish itself."[110]

'Listening to this narrow-minded objection, Jamsetjee said, "Well, Munshi Sahab, I quite agree with you there—the lamp should have no more oil than it can bear. But you see this young man does not wish that females should receive more knowledge than they want. He wants to give them a moderate education. So your illustration supports what he wishes."

'Munshi Sahab was in shock! Jamsetjee promised Naoroji that he would extend his support. In a few years, Jamsetjee opened four schools for Parsi girls in connection with his Benevolent Institution.'[111]

Perry clapped as Savitri and Jyoti smiled at how deftly Jamsetjee had handled the situation. 'What a wonderful story, Fatima. I am happy to see how well informed you are. Just like Jamsetjee, even the traders are coming forward in a big way. In Ahmedabad, the city's powerful Jain nagarsheth—the head merchant—is willing to help, while another wealthy benefactor, Maganbhai Karamchand, recently donated twenty thousand rupees to open two girls' schools.'

'That's a lot of money, Perry Sahab. Such donations will help us open many more schools here also,' Jyoti remarked.

Touched by the commitment of all those present, Erskine Perry immediately agreed to support two more schools to be set up by Jyoti. Inhabitants of Poona, Mr and Mrs Brown, also came forward to help. It was a very fruitful visit.

The awakening was well underway.

---

110 Dinyar Phiroze Patel, *Naoroji: Pioneer of Indian Nationalism*, (Harvard University Press, 2020).

111 'Religious & Social Reform', *Indu Prakash*, 23 March 1885, in Sorabji Bamanji Munshi to Naoroji, 1 March 1902, NAI, DNP, M-210 (25).

33

The Ceremony

Poona College Chowk, 12 February 1853

Four years into their work, Savitri, Fatima and Saraswati organized a prize distribution ceremony for the children of their schools. They wanted to conduct an open examination in public and show people the progress the girls had made.

The function was an unusual one; the British mingled both with the local elite[112] and the common folk. People had come with

112 As reported in M.G. Mali's book *Krantijyoti Savitribai Jyotirao Phule*, the following British guests were present at the function: Brigadier Tridel, Mrs Tridel, Mrs Cockburn, E.C. Jones, the Collector of Poona, Mrs Jones, Mrs Robbel, Major Candy, Captain Willoughby, Lieutenant Bannerman, Captain Morse, Mrs Morse, Dr Gillonds, Mrs Brown, Miss Hancock, Reverend James Mitchell, Mrs Mitchell, Reverend G.L. Feyton, Mrs Feyton, Reverend W.K. Mitchell, Professor Fraser, Mrs Fraser, R.T. Pinhe, E.S.A. Bossnet

mats to sit on, expecting a long function and entertainment. On one side of the college ground were seated all the girls of the various schools run by the Phule couple. On the other side were seated students of the Poona College.

Walvekar marvelled at the gathering. 'Have you ever seen such a large gathering, Govande?'

Govande shook his head in disbelief. 'This is like a festival!'

Tatya Saheb Bhide joined the two men. 'Jyoti has invited the collector, E.C. James, and his wife also today. But Revenue Commissioner Reeves[113] is not in town.'

Govande nodded. 'I cannot believe that we managed to get all these girls enrolled in school. I pinch myself sometimes.'

Walvekar teased, 'Maybe Saraswati Vahini can pinch you harder!'

Govande chided him, 'Stop fooling around. We have to welcome everyone. I see Brigadier Tridel and Mrs Tridel. Bhide Bhau, let us go welcome them. Walvekar, please tell all the volunteers to give the British guests only bread in case any of them ask for something to eat.'

Surprised, Walvekar asked, 'Arre Bhau, why just bread? Annasaheb Chiplunkar has organized a feast!'

---

and Professor McDougal. The following Indian guests were present at the function: Sardar Appasaheb Dhamdhere, Sardar Balasaheb Majumdar, Sardar Balasaheb Mehendale, Sardar Purshottam Sadashiv Biniwale, Sardar Daji Bhau Panse, Sardar Balasaheb Patwardhan, Sardar Rausaheb Khasgiwale, Sardar Krishnarao Tushibagwale, Deputy Collector Vinayakrao Vasudev, Annasaheb Chiplunkar, Professor Krushnashastri Chiplunkar, Professor Kero Laxman Chhatre, Judge Ardeshir Cursetji, teachers of the Poona college and Bhausaheb Shastri from Vadodara.

113 Revenue Commissioner H.W. Reeves was a generous patron of the girls' schools.

Govande explained, 'The Britishers won't eat anything other than bread. Last year, Sir William James Moore, the physician to the Queen, was sent to inspect the Poona Cantonment. He saw rice covered with flies and the cook-room swarming with even more flies. He thought the manner in which the meat was cooked was as if it were "food for dogs". Dr Moore was very unhappy with Indian cooks and proposed many changes. Which is why the British believe that milk and bread are the only two safe items to consume in Poona.'[114]

Walvekar looked stunned but decided to ensure that the English guests got only bread, with some butter perhaps.

Govande and Walvekar had no time to pursue this juicy conversation as an avalanche of crowds descended upon the venue. Almost two thousand people turned up, to the amazement of all; another thousand-odd were trying to see what was happening inside the college grounds from the nearby Vishrambaug Wada. Some of the guests were carrying musical instruments and there was revelry in the air.

Jyoti had been clear that neither he nor Savitri would address the gathering. Therefore, Annasaheb Chiplunkar, who had provided huge financial support to the schools, spoke about the need for society to understand the importance of the work begun by Jyotirao and carried on by Fatima and Savitri.

Fatima and Saraswati then brought a selection of girls to the stage and asked them a set of questions; it was akin to a brief exam to show what the girls had been learning. For the benefit of the English guests, Fatima asked the questions in English first and Marathi after.

---

114 C. Damle, 'Taste of Life: When Poona cantonment was one of the most hygienic stations in the British kingdom', *Hindustan Times*, 2 June 2022. The article talks about the above inspection and how bread and milk alone was deemed to be healthy.

'Chaya, come forward. If I loan you a hundred rupees and you have to pay me 15 per cent simple interest, how much money do you have to pay me after two years?' she asked gently.

'130 rupees,' said Chaya with her innocent eyes open wide, taking in the massive crowd gathered there. There was thunderous clapping when people realized that she had given the right answer. As the volunteers somehow managed to stop the claps, requesting the crowd to let the programme continue, Fatima moved on to the next question.

'Chakuli, come forward. What was the name of Chhatrapati Shivaji Maharaj's loyal dog and why do we remember its loyalty?'

Shakily responded confidently, in Marathi, 'Waghya. It was a unique dog and jumped into the pyre when Shivaji was burning.' Once again, the ground erupted into claps.

Next, Fatima called another young student, Jarna, forward. 'Can you recite the table of four?' she asked.

Jarna recited the table of four fluently.

Many people in the audience, who did not know how long a table was meant to be, kept clapping through the recitation.

And so on and so forth, all the girls answered Fatima's questions loudly[115] and correctly, to the delight and thunderous claps of the crowd. Mrs Jones, the collector's wife, gave away prizes to all the girls who were finishing their course.

'I congratulate you on your journey from zero to eighteen schools,' said Mrs Jones.

Thereafter, Major Candy, who was the chief guest, rose to address the gathering. 'That was quite a marvellous exposition!'

Looking at the young girls admiringly, Major Candy continued, 'I cannot believe that the history of India, which

115 Mics were not invented till 1876 by Emile Berliner while working with Thomas Edison and were patented by Graham Bell in 1878.

my esteemed fellow countryman James Mill wrote about, is transforming before my own eyes.'

As Major Candy heard applause from just a few people, he realized that his English speech had a limited audience.

Miss Brown, another donor to the schools, came forward and said, 'Thomas, are you going to give us a speech or join me for a dance with these lovely girls?'

Major Thomas Candy smiled in encouragement. Miss Brown surprised everyone by saying gaily, 'Girls, let us form a circle.'

Saraswati Govande stepped in to translate and helped the girls form a circle. Mrs Brown then stood right in the middle of all the girls and said, 'Repeat after me, girls,

They be at hand sir,
with stick and fiddle
They can play a new dance
Called hey diddle diddle!'[116]

Mrs Brown and Major Candy showed the girls simple dance steps. As they watched the girls learn dance steps, sing songs and laugh openly without fear, tears streamed down the faces of Savitri Phule and Fatima Sheikh.

A few more of the British guests who knew the song, joined the girls and Miss Brown. Many sang their favourite songs and danced.

The musicians in the crowd also joined in the fun. There was a common feeling of having achieved something, and for a moment, the idea of ruler and ruled, higher and lower castes all but disappeared into a much larger purpose—how to remove

116 A rhyme in Thomas Preston's 1569 play about the life of Cambyses, King of Persia.

the dark veil of ignorance that had been blinding the people of Poona for generations together.

A few months after this successful programme, in a meeting held in September 1853, Phule and his colleagues expressed their thanks to a wide variety of sources for their support—to the Board of Education, the Dakshina Prize Fund Committee, Mr Rivers, Mr Farrar, Gopal Hari Deshmukh, Vamanrao Janardan Ranade,[117] and the *Dnyanprakash*[118] (Marathi) and the *Vartamandipika*[119] (Marathi) newspapers.[120]

At the meeting, it was decided that even though a beginning had been made, it remained difficult to persuade the lower castes of the value of education for their children and that a lot more work remained to be done. Fatima suggested afterwards that offering the students school uniforms could also be explored. A set of clothes would be a wonderful incentive for children who were coming in wearing rags. This suggestion was welcomed by all.

117 This name is mentioned as a supporter by Rosalind O'Hanlon in *Caste Conflict and Ideology: Mahatma Jotirao Phule and Low Caste Protest in Nineteenth-Century Western India*, (Cambridge University Press, 1985).

118 Krishnaji Trymbak Ranade began publishing the Marathi newspaper *Dnyanprakash* from Poona on 12 February 1849. Initially, it was a weekly newspaper. It became a bi-weekly from 1853. For the duration of the Indian National Congress session at Poona in 1895, the newspaper was published daily with the aim of providing fresh news of the deliberations at the session. From August 1904, it became a regular daily newspaper.

119 A much smaller newspaper that competed with the *Prabhakar* for a brief period around 1852.

120 Reported in the *Dnyanodaya*, 15 July 1855.

'Jotirao [sic] was on intimate terms with the family of his friend Govande. Govande's wife Saraswatibai was a great friend of his wife Savitribai. Often these two friends Savitribai and Saraswatibai attended social functions together, had long chats and stayed at each other's house for hours at a time. Once Savitribai, who had gone to attend a marriage ceremony with her friend Saraswatibai, returned late in the evening. Jotirao did not see his friend's wife in company with his wife. He got angry with his wife for coming home late; but when he heard the voice of Saraswatibai Govande, he changed his tone and talked to her as if nothing had happened. Such was the respect he had for Govande and his wife.'[121]

121 Dhananjay Keer, *Mahatma Jyotirao Phuley*, (Popular Prakashan, 2012).

'I have heard that Candy Sahab has prepared many teachers and sent them from village to village to pass on their learning, but what is the use? All the Brahmins in these villages give secret advice to the Kunbis and Malis not to send their children to school.'

—Jyotirao Phule[122]

Facing page: When Savitri and Fatima took the children to school, they were physically confronted by many, including the Brahmins. Reproduced with permission from Azad Group of Publications.

122 Govind Chimnaji Bhate, *History of Modern Marathi Literature*, (A.V. Patwardhan, 1939).

PART 3

THE CONFLAGRATION

Section 10

Spectrum Thinking

A year before the celebrations at Poona College, Fatima and Savitri had many worries on their minds. Fatima was juggling her commitments to the garment business she had built with Usman. She began worrying about how empty Usman's life was and how she could change things. Savitri too worried about how the separation from his father had made Jyotirao bitter.

34

Women, Wishful Thinking, Worries

Fatima was not her usual bubbly self. She had observed how willing Miss Summer was to spend time with Usman and how he never encouraged her at all. There was no doubt that Usman would make a dependable partner for any woman. And yet, he seemed unwilling to enter into a relationship. She confided her worries to Savitri.

'Aapa, Bhaijaan is four years elder to me and I'm twenty-two. In our traditional terms, I'm too old to get married, and my worry is that Bhaijaan will also never experience the joys of a marriage. Right now, Khadija Bi and I cook and keep for him. But doesn't he deserve his own family?'

Savitri offered her perspective. 'Maybe he is waiting for you to get married first. Then he too can make a confident commitment.'

'Aapa, you forget that I am an engaged woman whose husband did not come to collect her.'

Savitri nodded. Fatima was so full of life that she muttered quietly under her breath, 'Thank God he didn't come!' Savitri heard it and smiled. The two of them had a bond so deep that they understood each other and laughed freely at each other.

Fatima added, 'To be honest, I have no recollection of my first marriage. Usman Bhai is the only one who remembers it. And Khadija Bi.' [123]

'What happened to you was your destiny,' said Savitri. 'But something new can happen too.'

The two of them were sitting together and correcting exam papers of the children.

'It is true that even I feel that Usman Bhai and Grace madam might be good together. Just imagine, her parents sent her here so she could find a groom, instead of fixing her marriage at the age of ten. I like the concept of growing up, having a choice,' continued Savitri.

Fatima was listening intently. 'Choice' was a heavy word. As it turned out, Grace Summer never found a suitable civil servant to get wedded to. She had returned to Poona even as Mrs Falkland had returned to Bombay. She was working alongside Fatima and Saraswati at the schools and would often give piano recitals on special occasions. She was an ally and brought books and fancy items like colour pencils for the children.

Fatima was in deep thought. 'Bhaijaan has a very deep mistrust of the British. I don't know whether he will emerge from it to see Grace madam for who she is. Just the other day,

---

123 According to Dr Benazeer Tamboli, 'Muslims from Lucknow were quite staunch. It is highly likely that Fatima got married before the age of ten. It was a practice that the groom's family would come and collect the girl post puberty. In Fatima's case, we can only surmise that no one came to collect her. That is why, after their parents died early, she continued to stay with her brother, Usman.'

he was telling Grace madam that the East India Company had cut off the thumbs of hundreds of weavers in Bengal to destroy the indigenous weaving industry in favour of British textile imports. Twenty weavers' families from Murshidabad and Nadia in Bengal then fled to Awadh. The nawab resettled them in the town of Mahua Dabar. My father knew some of those families. What surprised me was that Grace madam also spoke against the British atrocities.'

Savitri was glad. 'Even though Grace madam is an Angrez, I doubt she had anything to do with these sordid events.'

Fatima agreed, 'She doesn't, and Bhaijaan cannot paint all the Angrez with the same brush. The Prophet himself has said, "If a Christian woman enters a Muslim household, she shall be received with kindness, and she shall be given the opportunity to pray in her church; there shall be no dispute."'[124]

'What a lovely thought,' said Savitri, a faraway look in her eyes. 'We are not in very different circumstances right now. You are not able to express your concern to Usman. I am not able to express my concern to Govindrao Dada. His deteriorating health is a matter of immense worry for Shetji. He blames himself for Dada's condition and the fact that we left home.'

Fatima checked herself. It seemed that she was always ranting to Aapa but never being a listener. 'That is not fair, Aapa. You left home so that Bhattji and Purohitji would not trouble Dada every day!'

'It's not that, Fatima. Even Saguna Aau is defying Dada's wishes. She has started looking after the Meethganj school. She gets exhausted with all the work she is doing—her domestic duties, managing the farm and the school. Add to that, Dada

124 Prophet Muhammad, 'The Covenant of the Prophet Muhammad with the Monks of Mount Sinai.'

screams at her because there is no one else to vent at! When it becomes unbearable, Aau comes here to talk. Shetji also asks me every day, "Has Dada sent any message?" I think he is secretly hoping that one day Dada will ask him to come back home,' Savitri mused.

'How angry can a father be with his son? Deep down, Dada must still love Jyoti Bhaijaan. Have faith in Allah and ask Jyoti Bhaijaan to go and meet Dada,' Fatima offered.

Hesitantly, Fatima continued, 'I think Jyoti Bhaijaan's guilt is a bit deeper than you think. The other day, he was telling us that he blames himself for how lonely you have become. Your brother does not talk to you, no one comes to meet you from Naigaon any more; your father-in-law also does not talk to you. He thinks he has eroded your relationships and taken all the joys of a family away from you,' said Fatima with the frankness that can only be expected from a true friend.

'Really? I had no idea,' said Savitri. 'Besides, how many women around us know the joy of a family? Not the Brahmin women. Not the Shudra women. The only women we see liberated are the wives of Angrez officers and some missionary couples. I have never complained to Shetji about anything.'

'But he observes and he cares, Aapa. Perhaps you could give him the courage to take a step towards repairing his relationship with his father? We must close all wounds in time, lest they degenerate to the point where you have to amputate them.'

Savitri nodded, grateful for the kind words. The two women locked the school, having finished their work for the day and walked home.

Meanwhile, with his father's health on a downswing, Jyoti was also weighed down by many thoughts. On the one hand, he realized he had to step in to manage his father's workload. But that was just an excuse to reconnect. Savitri counselled her husband that it was the duty of the son to take care of his father in his old age. And anything negative that Govindrao said at this time should not be taken to heart. So Jyotirao slowly worked his way back into his father's life.

The Brahmin influence over Govindrao had also waned because they now realized that pressuring Govindrao wasn't going to help. Jyoti had already sparked a revolution, and there was no going back on that. However, Jyoti did not get much time with his father towards the end. Savitri realized that this would become a bone of contention for him—Jyoti would always blame the Brahmins for this.

Govindrao died a happy man in the company of his family in 1852.

35

Savitri Finds New Problems to Solve

Even as Fatima and Savitri were grappling with myriad personal issues, they knew that they had barely scratched the surface, when it came to educating girls. Savitri wanted to talk to the parents of the girls who had not yet not enrolled in school; also, of those who were enrolled but not allowed to attend.

So one day, she invited two of the committee members of the schools, Vishnushastri Pandit and Keshav Bhawalkar, to visit. Saraswati and Fatima were also present when she took the opportunity to broach an important topic.

'I need your help, Fatima. I want you to take over as the headmistress of the schools.'

'Savitri Aapa, you are the headmistress. How can I replace you?'

'Fatima, you are not replacing me but relieving me. One of us needs to tour the villages nearby, asking more and more girls to join our schools. I want to understand why families are not sending their girls; find ways to persuade them.'

Fatima understood. All present clapped for the new headmistress as Fatima hid her face in her hands in embarrassment. 'Savitri Aapa, you have made me the happiest person in the world. I don't know anyone else in my community who has ever become a headmistress.'

Saraswati came forward to hug Fatima. 'You deserve it,' she said.

'You know,' Fatima continued, 'I feel that people want us to succeed. But we have to make a few rules. We must ask families to stop sending girls with heavy jewellery to the schools. One girl almost got robbed.'

Vishnushastri Pandit nodded vigorously, 'Yes. The Lokkes are sending their daughter-in-law fully decked up so that she can project their status. They're also sending a servant with her. How will the girl ever be accepted by the other girls who are coming here barefoot?'

'I will talk to them about this,' Savitri assured them. 'What I want your support with, Bhau, is that I have been thinking of starting a mahila seva mandal.'

Keshav, who had known Savitri for long, knew that something like this was coming. She would never rest till she was able to enrol and teach more girls. He looked at Savitri, all ears.

'Bhau, We have to move on all fronts. You know Shetji has also started a society for increasing education amongst Mahars, Mangs and others.[125] Yesterday, he reached out to his Mang

125 The society for increasing education amongst Mahars, Mangs and others was started in 1853. Sadashiv Ballal Govande was appointed president, Moro Vitthal Walvekar was to be the secretary and Sakharam Yasavant Paranjpe was to be the treasurer.

watchman Raanba[126] to convince him to send his children to school. Fortunately, Raanba agreed and he's galvanizing more people to send their children as well.'

Fatima also had good news to share. 'Three more teachers are finishing their training this week, from our first batch of girls at Bhidewada. They can take over the running of this school.'

'This is wonderful news, but we also need money; hopefully our purpose has enough merit to attract some big donors,' said Savitri.

Pandit added, 'Savitri Vahini, Walvekar has written a letter to the Bombay government[127] asking for money to build a proper school and for land to build it on. In his letter, he has explained the miserable condition of the lower castes.' He removed the letter from his bag and read out, 'The lower castes are sunk deep in ignorance and misery, arising from want of education and intercourse with society in general.' He has worded it well and we will surely get some help.'

The group expressed their appreciation for the letter.

Saraswati then asked, 'Savitri Tai[128], tell me a little more about your vision for the mahila seva mandal.' Saraswati was in awe of Savitri and Fatima. She felt fortunate to be in the same room as them and to be able to contribute in some way. And her euphonious voice, with which she would tirelessly read Savitribai's poems of awakening[129] to vast gatherings of women,

---

126 This incident is narrated in Dr Ravindra Thakur (translated into English by Reshma Kulkarni Pathare), *Mahatma Jyotirao Phule*, (Mehta Publishing House, 2020).

127 Moro Vitthal Walvekar to Viscount Falkland, 16 December 1853, Bombay Public Consultations, General Department, 13-30 September 1854, nos. 5411 to 5417.

128 'Tai' means elder sister in Marathi.

129 See Annexure 8.

added a softer aspect to the protest against the exploitation of the womenfolk.

Savitri spoke with great care, 'Saraswati, as you know, Fatima and I got educated with the help of the Mission; maybe many locals think that we have changed and are not "their own" people. I want to celebrate our culture and explain the link between education and emancipation in a way they understand.'

Fatima understood immediately. 'That's true, Aapa. But isn't it also true that many people make helplessness a part of their identity? They want to sit idly and blame their circumstances. How do we give these women the motivation to change things?'

Keshav said eagerly, 'Fatima Bibi, you are absolutely right. It is difficult to reform those who have no desire to change their circumstances. The Mahars and Mangs and other Atishudras also must agree to become a part of their own awakening in a conscious way.'

It was decided that Saraswati would help Savitri start the mahila seva mandal and Fatima would continue running the schools.

In her subsequent well-known speech on vidyadaan (knowledge donation), Savitribai Phule explored the dialogical nature of the teaching–learning processes, in which the learner was not a passive recipient but an active agent.

36

The Mahila Seva Mandal Takes Shape

To begin the establishment of the mahila seva mandal, Savitri wrote a letter inviting all the women of the neighbourhood to join her for a small gathering on the occasion of Makar Sankranti, the Hindu harvest festival that marks the end of winter. Her larger aim was to nurture their consciousness about their social status and rights.

Savitri's language reflects her passion for equality:[130]

> The gathering will take place on 13/01/1852 in the presence of the president of this help group, Mrs Jones. All women should bring their daughters and daughters-in-law along with them for the programme. It would

130 The contents of this letter feature in Akhileshwari Ramagoud and Simhadri Somanaboina (eds), *The Routledge Handbook of the Other Backward Classes in India: Thought, Movements and Development*, (Taylor & Francis, 2001).

be at five o'clock in the evening. The women belonging to any religion or caste would be seated on one carpet without any kind of discrimination and sweets would be distributed to all equally.

Fatima, Savitri and Saraswati Govande received the guests. The programme was a traditional one, called haldi-kumkum.[131] Makar Sankranti also involves a kite-flying festival, wherein the people celebrate by giving each other til (sesame) laddoos and wish each other that the sweetness of the laddoos spread to their words as well.

Saraswati Govande spoke at the event. 'We are grateful to Mrs Jones, our chief guest, Savitri Tai for organizing this event and Fatima Bibi for running the schools and freeing up Savitri Tai to do this work. Today is a day when all women have come forward to recognize that we are all equal by birth. There is no difference in our bodies and no difference in our minds. The only difference between two people is what they are capable of doing. And with education, we can bridge this difference too.'

Savitri also addressed the gathering. 'Let us teach each other whatever we know. Fatima taught me how to make blankets from scrap cloth. I can teach you how to spin cloth and make sarees, so that you can all earn some money of your own. Anyone who can teach anything to others must come forward. All of you must also join the schools and make your daughters join with you!'

Everyone clapped. People knew that Savitri was not an idle orator, she was a doer. Fatima had set up a table on the side to enrol more women in their schools.

---

131 The haldi-kumkum ceremony is a social gathering in which married women exchange haldi (turmeric) and kumkum (vermilion powder) as symbols of their married status and wish for their husbands' long lives.

As all the women sat together on the same carpet, sans any caste-based segregation, Savitri came forward to offer haldi and kumkum, and Mrs Jones gave everyone a til laddoo. This was a landmark event, in which the Kunbis sat next to the Atishudras without a murmur.

Over the next few months, under the aegis of the Mahila Seva Mandal, Savitri took up the issue of forcible tonsuring of widows among the Hindus. She launched a campaign urging barbers not to cut the hair of widows. In those days, the situation of upper-caste widows was heart-wrenching. All women, after the death of the husband, were required to shave their heads, regardless of their age. The Brahmins strictly followed this cruel custom, which had been handed down since the time of the Peshwas. Widows would not show their face due to the humiliation of having a shaven head.

Thanks to the efforts of Savitri, many barbers took an oath to stop tonsuring widows, and this came to be known as the famous barbers' strike.[132] Imagine a large number of barbers taking a financial hit and enthusiastically joining a movement against the physical or mental torture of women. Such was the respect Savitri enjoyed.

---

132 Dr Rajabhau Chhaganrao Korde and Dr Chetana Vishwanth Rao Doglikar, 'Social, Cultural and Educational Perspectives of Women', lulu.com, 2019.

37

Fatima's Travails

It was not easy being Fatima. In her own community, she had few friends.

Structurally, the Muslim community was somewhat different from the rest of the locals in Poona, even though the social condition of Muslim women at the time wasn't very different from that of lower castes; lack of female education and social disapproval of female autonomy were common threads. The preference for male offspring was also common to both Hindus and Muslims (especially Muslim rulers, who desired only male offspring). Early marriages were encouraged as well.

There were many differences too. Just as Sati was a uniquely Hindu practice, there were several unique discriminatory practices against Muslim women, such as unilateral divorce by men.[133] Divorce was effective orally or in writing, without any witness. Husbands were liable to pay maintenance to the divorced wife. The practice of khula, whereby a woman could seek divorce, existed too, although this was subject to the willingness of the husband to grant his wife a divorce.

Polygamy was practised within the Mughal royalty. Muslim women in polygamous marriages lived with their co-wives in the royal harem. This percolated to other social strata too.

The practice of purdah and its social restrictions presented Muslim women with an additional challenge in overcoming their subordination within family, community and society.

The thinking around women's education in particular was influenced by educators like Syed Ahmed Khan, the founder of the Aligarh Muslim University, who said, 'There could be no satisfactory education ... for Muhammedan females until a large number of Muhammedan males [had] received a sound education.'[134]

Sadly, Sir Syed's vision of modern education for Muslims did not put women first.

Further, the ulema, the Muslim theologians who interpreted Qura'nic verses, had a certain position on women. This was based on the notion of women as 'fitna', those responsible for causing unrest or mutiny.

Accordingly, women's social interactions with men had to be limited, which in effect translated into a control over female sexuality and female seclusion from public places.

---

133 S. Kazi, *Muslim Women in India*, (Minority Rights Group, February 1999).

134 Ayesha Jalal, 'The convenience of subservience: Women and the state of Pakistan', in D. Kandiyoti (ed.), *Women, Islam and the State*, (London: Macmillan, 1991).

Given that Fatima was liberal and free-spirited, one can possibly surmise that both Muslims and orthodox Hindus opposed her as much as they opposed Savitri. Particularly, fathers of Muslim girls preferred that her non-purdah existence and unmarried status be kept out of the lives of their daughters.

Usman never explained Fatima's choices to anyone. She was his greatest pride and greatest duty.

But fate had its own ways…

This was a time before Jyoti's father Govindrao's death. This incident is mentioned in M.G. Mali's *Krantijyoti Savitribai Jyotirao Phule.*

It had been many years since Savitri and Jyoti's marriage. Yet, they did not have a child. So Govindrao suggested that Jyoti could perhaps marry again. Relatives and friends seemed to agree that in order to preserve the lineage, Jyoti must find another partner who could bear him a child.

Despite the fact that Jyoti did not show any interest in the matter, certain developments took a life of their own. Fathers of beautiful daughters started secretly hoping that Jyoti would choose them over Savitri. When Savitri realized that matters had taken a serious turn, she told Jyoti without batting an eyelid, 'If you feel you must marry again, then I have no objection!'

This period was like a trial by fire for Savitri. One can presume that she was aghast at the very idea; however, since the proposals were coming for Jyoti, she promptly left the decision in his hands.

Jyoti was livid at the proposals. He said, 'If I have a right to marry a second time, Savitri should also have the same right. Why should only a man marry multiple times? Why not a woman?'

The horde of proposals promptly disappeared!

Section 11

The Will to Sacrifice

The anecdote narrated earlier is one of many instances that prove that Savitri, Jyotirao and their many co-workers had an unshakeable sense of righteousness and always put the interests of others above their own.

On the personal front, Fatima kept herself so busy that she had no time to think about what she was missing. Yet, at times, she would look at the relationship that Savitri and Jyotirao shared and wish for the same companionship for Usman.

Sometimes for herself too.

38

Changing Tides, Changing Climes

Khadija Bi had long been the caretaker of Fatima and Usman's house. When Savitri and Jyotirao came to stay, her workload increased beyond her liking. A widow who had been living under Usman's benefaction for most of her life, Khadija remained orthodox in her ways.

She felt that her own daughter was better off than Fatima, who remained unmarried. Fatima's work towards educating girls went against her traditional ideas of right and wrong. Khadija Bi had tried to influence Fatima, but the latter's spirit was too independent to be quelled.

When Savitri made Fatima the headmistress of the schools, Usman was very proud of his sister. But Khadija Bi felt things had gone too far in the name of revolution.

On top of all this, Grace Summer had started visiting their house frequently. Clearly, Usman and Grace had a fondness for each other, and this was unacceptable to Khadija. A Jhulaha would marry a Christian! Hai rabba!

Khadija became withdrawn and morose on most days, and it showed in her work. Ever since Usman and Fatima had decided to get involved in social work, they had even more visitors and she felt that she could not cope with their demands anymore.

One day, Savitri, Usman, Fatima, Grace Summer and Jyotirao were seated at the Sheikhs' house. Something was troubling Savitri.

'I met the widow Parvati today; she is in very bad shape. The men in her own family, including her brothers-in-law, father-in-law and others, exploit her physically. Now she is pregnant, and she doesn't know who the father is. Her family is disowning her. Parvati is left with only two options: to either commit suicide or abort her illegitimate child. The way in which widows are forced to abort an illegitimate child is so dangerous, they can die.'

Jyotirao asked, 'What is stopping you from helping Parvati, Savitri?'

'I have been thinking, Shetji. Fatima has been running the schools with Saraswati's help, and she finally has a good number of teachers. Along with the Mahila Seva Mandal, I want to start a home for the prohibition of infanticide among these abused widows.'[135]

Usman offered, 'I think space can be managed. We will need donors and doctors, and we will also need police protection for the home.'

Grace chipped in, 'How can I help?'

'Madam, you can spend time with the widows and teach them some new skills. You have so many gifts,' urged Fatima.

Usman nodded approvingly.

---

135 On 28 January 1853, Savitri Phule opened an Infanticide Prohibition Home—the first of its kind in India. In this home, widows could give birth to their children and leave them there. Sixty-six women gave birth to their children in that shelter up to 1873. This was a great social service done by Savitribai at that time—in the dark ages.

Jyotirao thought of Devrao Thosar, who could arrange for police protection. Fatima offered to arrange for teachers to make the women literate and teach them embroidery.

Savitri was joyous. 'Arre waah! We have found all the solutions in our house!'

Khadija Bi was listening to all this. Savitri and Jyotirao had cleared out a room in their own house for the unfortunate widow Parvati to sleep in for a few nights.

Khadija Bi felt a pit in her stomach about her petty complaints regarding the increased workload at home, at a time when the people sitting before her did not bat an eyelid before agreeing to help others with no expectations in return. And their concern for the plight of widows struck a chord with her. She spoke, to everyone's surprise.

'Why do you want to help this widow?'

'One doesn't have a choice when it comes to helping those less fortunate!' said Jyoti, smiling.

Khadija Bi persisted, 'But people say that people like you are destroying your own traditions.'

Jyotirao laughed. 'Yes, Khadija Bi, they do, but I have a very convenient habit. I forget all the insults people hurl at me. I only remember the lessons. Let me tell you about the time I was insulted and asked to leave a Brahmin friend's wedding, due to my caste. When I returned home that night, I was deeply shaken.[136] I asked my father to help me understand. He turned around and told me that it was a lifelong lesson for me to not cross the lines of right and wrong. But I did not agree with my father. Instead, I decided that such injustice must not happen to anybody else and started working towards it.'

---

136 Dhananjay Keer, *Mahatma Jyotirao Phuley*, (Popular Prakashan, 2012).

'They were unkind to you. Mohammad says, "Kindness is a mark of faith, and whoever has not kindness has not faith,"' said Khadija Bi.

'In that case, Khadija Bi, we must all accept that Usman and Fatima are full of faith,' said Jyotirao.

Khadija nodded quietly.

Grace was smiling at Usman.

Jyotirao wondered aloud, 'Grace madam, other than our very capable friend Usman here, what keeps you busy in Poona?'

Everyone joined in the laughter.

Grace said with open admiration, 'People search for something to do their entire lives, Jyotirao. Here, you folks can't seem to stop working for the good of others! There's no other place I'd rather be!'

The gathering dispersed. One can only hope that the young reformers won over Khadija Bi's heart that day.

39

Savitri, the Wife

Savitribai had a very unique quality; she would always consider all aspects of any situation and offer the right counsel. No one knew this better than Jyotirao.

Sometime during 1853–54, Jyotirao quarrelled with his colleagues and resigned from the school management committee due to a difference of opinion on the curriculum. Several historians suggest that Jyotirao had developed extreme views and that he disagreed with other members of the committee over the extent to which the Brahmins should be held responsible both for the condition of the low castes and for the backwardness of Hindu society itself. The rest of the committee members had a less radical view than him on this.

Savitri knew that Jyotirao's personal grudge against the Brahmins had only been intensified after his father's death. But she never forgot that her advice must not be biased.

'Shetji, you're looking very agitated today.'

'Savitri, what is it that you do not know? These Brahmins kept me away from my unwell father. I could not even tend to him when he was unwell. They pelted stones and cow dung at you. They did everything possible to prevent my education. They killed Ghollay's daughter, and they continue to think that women from lower castes should dance privately for their entertainment. These are the people, Savitri, who have ruled our minds for generations! Because I see them clearly and I fight openly, does that make my views extreme?'

'You may see them clearly, Shetji. But before that you need to see yourself clearly. There is an entire army of teachers that has now been created. They are looking to you for guidance. Is your hatred against Brahmins so powerful that you are prepared to give up your love for progress? If you resign over your own radical views, where does that leave them?'

Jyotirao looked at Savitri, exasperated. Why did she always have to be right?

'If you look back five hundred years, the villains were different. Two hundred years ago, again they were different. So even if you're blaming the Brahmins and others are not, it's because history is not that simple.'

Jyotirao nodded. Savitri came and sat next to him.

'You have to continue teaching, even if it's just for two hours a day. Others can run the schools, but your involvement gives everyone energy,' she implored.

Jyotirao heeded Savitri's advice and took a job as a part-time teacher in 1854, in the Scottish Mission School for female boarders. His recruitment was reported in the *Oriental Christian Spectator* in February 1855 as follows:

> We have been happy in securing the aid in their instruction for nearly four hours a day one of the most zealous and

> accomplished teachers in Pune—Jotee Govind Rao Phoolay—a native philanthropist, whose … efforts on behalf of the education of females and the low castes have called forth the warmest commendation of the Board of Education and of Government itself. He has fulfilled our highest expectations; the progress of the girls has been most satisfactory.

Phule had maintained contact with the Scottish missionaries after he had completed his education. He had used the mission facilities in the course of his own educational work, if not for anything else, just to access books and newspapers from all over the world. Savitri was right to point out that Jyotirao's continuance as a teacher gave others courage. It was because of his influence that one of the Dalit students, eleven-year-old Muktabai, wrote a powerful essay in 1855 titled *'Mang Maharachya Dukhvisayi'*.[137]

Muktabai's essay was ferocious in its condemnation of Brahmins. In particular, she singled out the elitism of Brahminic religious values: these constituted 'a religion that one person alone can enjoy, while the rest of mankind looks on with hungry faces'. She reasoned in her essay,

> Now apparently, if the Vedas are only for the Brahmins, they are obviously not for us. If the Vedas belong only to the Brahmins, then it is an open secret that we do not have the Book. We are without the Book—we are without any religion. If the Vedas are for the Brahmins only, then we are not bound to act according to the Vedas. If merely looking at the Vedas can get us into grievous sins (as the

137 The full text of the essay is provided in Annexure 5.

> Brahmins claim), then would not following them be the height of foolishness?

This gives us a valuable insight into the development of Phule's ideas, and in particular into the tone of teaching that the committee found hard to accept.

Jyoti and Savitri continued to open institutions and charitable organizations. In 1855, they opened a night school for farmers and labourers so that they could work during the day and attend school at night.

One night as they were sitting and having dinner, Jyoti noticed that Savitri's face had softened. She said, 'Fatima has been taking excellent care of the schools. But we will have to groom Saraswati Govande to take over soon. I believe Fatima has finally met someone whom she wants to marry.'

Jyotirao was overjoyed with the news.

'How long have you known? Does Usman know?'

'I found out when I accidentally opened a letter addressed to her. I don't think Fatima has told anyone about this yet.'

Jyotirao continued smiling. Fatima was the sister he had never had. He wanted to immediately share this news with Baig Sahab. But Savitri cautioned him to give it some time till Fatima herself was ready to talk.

In the meantime, overburdened with work, Savitri fell seriously ill and went to Naigaon to build a bridge of understanding with her brother. During this period, a letter that Savitri wrote to Jyotirao expresses how much she was struggling to reform her own brother's mind. [138]

138 The full text of this letter is provided in Annexure 7.

40

Blessings in the Form of Barkat

Once Savitri returned from her travels, she wanted to attend to the matter of Fatima's amour. Baig Sahab was taken into confidence first. Savitri met him and told him about a young man named Barkat who wanted to wed Fatima. She suggested that he should get to know him and find a way to introduce him to Usman.

Baig Sahab was more than up to the task. He invited Barkat home, spent some time with him and then announced that a visit to Usman's shop for chai was long overdue.

Upon spotting Baig Sahab, Muhasibji smiled from ear to ear while also welcoming the young guest with him.

Baig hailed him, 'Chetori (how are you), Muhasibji?'

It seemed that Baig Sahab was in a good mood indeed.

'Khairiyat, Baig Sahab.'

'Where is Usman? I have brought a special friend with me today, Muhasibji. Meet Barkat Miyaan.'

'*Barkat Miyaan, tashreef rakhiye,*' said the affable Muhasib.

Usman was in the godown behind the shop, loading a few trucks. When he returned to the shop, he was delighted to see Baig Sahab.

'Khosh amadid, Usman. Meet Barkat Miyaan. He has Farsi blood in his veins and runs a khanekhaaz (hotel) in Agra,' said Baig.

'Khosh amadid, Barkat Miyaan. Agra is where we are originally from! What brings you here? And what are you carrying in your hands?' asked Usman.

'This is a rare copy of Ghulam Husain Khan Tabatabai's *Siyar Al Mutakhirin*,[139] a history of modern times. It is a highly appreciated work. Have you read it, Usman Miyaan?' asked Barkat.

Muhasibji came forward to examine the book as Barkat continued.

'Ghulam Husain has written about the history of the Mahomedan power in India. I am told that James Mill referred to this when he wrote his book *The History of British India* and that Janaab Macaulay appreciated it.'

'So finally, Baig Sahab, we have found someone who talks just like you! How come you own a khanekhaaz, Barkat Miyaan? Shouldn't you own a bookstore?' quizzed Muhasib.

'Look around you, Muhasibji. Would you not agree that our community has excelled in certain professions? Agricultural expertise, forms of trade and of course, healing. It seems I am good at nothing. My walid sahab had a big haveli, which I converted into a khanekhaaz. I hope that Baig Sahab will tell me which paintings, books and letters I must keep for guests in my khanekhaaz,' said Barkat with humility.

---

139 This book is believed to have been written around 1780.

Baig added, 'Barkat Miyaan works with the British here. He helps organize tours to the Taj Mahal for wealthy foreigners. He wants to use some of that money to buy his poor Gaffar Chacha's books.'

Usman was thrilled to meet a progressive young man like Barkat. He was also happy to note that Barkat knew how to maintain cordial relations with the British. The conversation and laughter continued till late.

Khadija Bi brought sheer korma for the guests.

Barkat was determined to make a good impression on Usman. He had met Fatima nearly five years ago at Mrs Koofter's house. It so happened that the new lieutenant-general of the Agra Presidency[140] was to invite a few dignitaries from Bombay to visit the Taj Mahal in Agra, and Barkat's khanekhaaz in Agra was identified as the preferred place for them to stay.

Mrs Koofter was to give Barkat a list of dietary dos and don'ts for this trip, so she had invited him to her home to discuss the matter. She had also invited Fatima as she wanted her to make her some light summer day-dresses. It was in the waiting room of Mrs Koofter's residence that Barkat and Fatima met each other.

Fatima had guessed that Barkat was from Agra. When Barkat confirmed that he was, she had started chatting non-stop. She shared her childhood memories of Agra. Then she spoke about her work to build schools in Poona with Savitri.

---

140 In 1833 an act of Parliament was passed to constitute a new presidency (province), with its capital at Agra. But this scheme was never fully carried out, and in 1835 another statute authorized the appointment of a lieutenant-governor for the North-Western Provinces.

Mrs Koofter finally called them in and instantly took pity on poor Barkat. 'Are you all right, young man? Fatima can talk the hind leg off a donkey!'

Barkat, however, said that he had kept enchanted company in the waiting room.

Truth be told, he was swept off his feet.

Far from any affectations of shyness, Fatima had given him her address in Agra and asked him to go check on her old house. Was it still there? Barkat had promised to check. Fatima had also asked him to keep her posted about any new Farsi writings and books. Barkat had promised again.

Fatima was pleasantly surprised to receive letters, books and small paintings from Barkat from time to time. She wrote back, telling him about her marriage at a young age, how her brother meant everything to her and that she was enjoying her work in the schools.

Barkat increased the frequency of his visits to Bombay in the hope that he would get to see Fatima more often. She always obliged, partly because of her natural open nature and partly because of her readiness to consider another life, so that Usman might find companionship too.

Eventually, Fatima had asked Barkat to visit formally with Baig Sahab and Savitri Aapa and share his intention to marry her. They would take care of everything else. This was an important visit as Barkat was on a marriage mission.

The day after meeting Baig Sahab and Usman, Barkat visited Jyotirao and Savitri.

'Jyoti Bhaijaan, we need you to come to Agra and open some more schools there. You are Khuda's own messenger.'

Savitri had a twinkle in her eyes. She clearly favoured Barkat as one would favour a son-in-law.

'Bhau, please be open and tell Shetji why you're really here! Don't expect him to divine your intentions.'

Barkat was blushing. Just then, a young boy entered the house and said, 'Tatya,[141] we have run out of slates and chalk. Teacher asked me to come and get more.'

Jyotirao smiled, 'Take them from that big sack in the corner. How many do you need?'

The boy said he needed seven and took the supplies from the sack.

Jyotirao muttered, 'With some luck, we will get some more slates and chalk tomorrow.'

Barkat picked up on the luck bit, saying, 'Do you believe in luck, Bhaijaan? I do.'

'My father used to. When I was small, the village pandit came home one day. He told my father that if he placed flowers in a small, faraway, neglected temple for ten days, then he would get a very big order. My father was excited, and since he could not make the long journey, he asked me to do it on his behalf. At the end of ten days, he did get the promised order—from Maha Pandit Bhattji—and was overjoyed. But I told him that it was all a farce. That I had not placed the flowers in the temple on even a single day.

'My father scolded me. "What is this maskari?" he asked.

'I said, "Dada, don't you see, I never offered the flowers! All of this is a lie. The pandit doesn't know anything more than you and I. He was going to give you the order anyway. He didn't even check whether you were placing flowers in that temple."

'My father was livid. He thundered, "How dare you play with dharma? Shastriji was right. No school for you from tomorrow."

141 The children Jyoti taught referred to him as 'Tatya'.

'My father was gullible. Now he's no more. I had a mother figure in my life, Sagunabai. She negotiated with my father for my education and my freedom by getting me married to Savitri.'

Barkat nodded. 'Huzoor, then you too should believe in luck!'

This brought a smile to everyone's face.

Barkat continued, 'Perhaps your blessings could make me a lucky man too!'

Jyotirao looked at Savitri and again at Barkat. He seemed completely lost.

'Shetji, Barkat Bhau wants to marry Fatima Bibi. He is seeking your blessings!'

Jyotirao was overjoyed; he asked, 'Is Fatima willing? Has Usman agreed?'

'Shetji, Fatima and Barkat Bhau have been writing to each other for more than five years now. Even Baig Sahab has given his blessings. Now we all need to do is to talk to Usman.'

'Then there is nothing to wait for. Am I the last to know? What about your parents, Barkat?' asked Jyoti.

'I lost them when I was young,' said Barkat with the hint of a pain that hadn't subsided with time.

'Savitri, we must go and talk to Usman,' declared Jyoti.

That evening Jyotirao and Savitri took Barkat's proposal to Usman's house. Usman wept, overwhelmed at the thought that his sister was finally going to get married and that too, to a man of God who had built something of his own.

Soon after, the good news was shared with all. Khadija Bi had already been asked to prepare a feast that night.

Savitri thought of the time when she had opened Barkat's letter by mistake and discovered the happy bond that he and Fatima shared. Fatima was bashful as a bride-to-be now! Rightfully so.

Jyotirao and Savitri were present to offer their blessings at the ensuing marriage proceedings, after which Fatima went to Agra with Barkat,[142] to become the barkat in his life. One can safely presume that Savitri's band of crusaders,[143] Saraswati Govande and Miss Grace Summer, were present at the wedding too, as was all of Poona. It was as if the entire city was bidding farewell to its favourite daughter.

In Conclusion

So, what happened to Savitri and Fatima's schools? A total of eighteen schools were opened, not just for girls but for other underprivileged people as well. While the dates of when which school was shut down and for what reason are not available,

142 Syed Naseer Ahmed (translated into English from Telugu by B.V.K. Purnanandam), *The First Muslim Woman Teacher of Modern India-Fatima Shaik*, (Azad House of Publications). Excerpt from page 50:

'What happened to Fatima Sheikh after 1856? As an answer to this question Dr. Shamshuddin Tamboli, a historian from Pune, declared that she got married and that Jyotirao Phule and Savithribai Phule performed that wedding. In *Muslim Sathyashodhak*, a paper published under his editorship, he has narrated this in a detailed way. He has also narrated that Phule couple themselves performed that dowry-less ideal wedding.'

Dr Shamshuddin also quotes Mr. S.M. Mushreef, former director-general of police, who revealed this in his foreword to the book, *Bharathatheel Pahili Musalman Shikshak: Fathima Shaik* by the renowned writer of Meeraz, Maharashtra, Dinakar Vishnu Kakade. Further, Dinakar Vishnu Kakade and Dr Shamshuddin revealed that Fatima Sheikh had moved to her in-laws' place after the wedding and on account of this no details of her life have been available. In the absence of any authoritative evidence to this piece of information, its authenticity is yet to be confirmed.

143 There is no definite date available for the death of Saguna Kshirsagar.

what is known is that these schools had a massive impact. They were a slap in the face of orthodoxy.

What is documented in several books is that by 1858 some of schools had shut down and the rest were handed over to others to manage. There were several reasons for this.

Firstly, it would seem that neither Savitri nor Jyoti imagined that they would run these schools all their lives. They were institution-builders; there were several problems they wanted to solve. They wanted to institutionalize the education of both girls and the underprivileged Mahars, Mangs, Shudras and Atishudras by starting a movement. Their reason for opening these schools, therefore, was to help the underprivileged and downtrodden understand their rights as human beings.

Secondly, it is recorded that Fatima Sheikh got married somewhere after 1856.[144] She was an important third pillar of this exercise of education. She was not just a teacher but also a trainer and a headmistress. Her departure would have created a vacuum. Moreover, there is no evidence to suggest whether Saguna Aau was alive at this time or that Saraswati Govande continued to help run the schools.

Thirdly, private European donations started drying up post the Indian Rebellion of 1857.

So, what do we know for sure? One of the Phule schools was converted into the government-run Female Training College. Margaret Mitchell was appointed as the superintendent.[145] Two more schools were taken over by the Education Department

144 Dinakar Vishnu Kakade, *Bharathatheel Pahili Musalman Shikshak: Fathima Shaik*, (Sanghamithra Publications, 2019).

145 Director of Public Instruction, 1864–41; testimony of Vithabai Sakharam Chowdari, Headmistress Bhavnagar School, in Indian Education Commission. Bombay Provincial Committee, Evidence and Memorials (II)

and incorporated into the Female Training College's system of superintendence.[146] A few others were shut down.

However, the schools, though short-lived, changed mindsets forever. Mama Parmanand, a devoted soldier of social justice and political teacher spoke about this, 'When a Maratha teaches his own wife and asks her to teach other Brahmin girls, it is nothing short of a revolution. But what is even more revolutionary is when she teaches Mahars and Mangs and gives them the confidence that they're key pillars of society—this is nothing short of entering a hungry lion's den.'

The full impact of the social reformation movement can perhaps only be realized and not measured. It is not accurately documented how many of the girls and lower-caste children from the Phule schools became teachers themselves. However, in 1882, when the Indian Education Commission was appointed to examine general elementary education,[147] a few experts were invited to opine on why the educational policy had failed.

One of these expert practitioners was Vithabai Sakharam Chowder,[148] a Shudra girl who had begun her education in one of the schools set up by Fatima and Savitri. Vithabai had gone on to teach and spread the light. However, one can safely surmise that she was not the only one. She is known because she testified.

One might presume that many more took the light within them to faraway places across India and the rest of the world.

146 Ibid.

147 Tim Allender, 'Learning abroad: the colonial educational experiment in India, 1813–1919', *Paedagogica Historica* 45, no. 6, 2009, pp. 727–741, 738.

148 Ulrike Lindner and Dörte Lerp (eds), *New Perspectives on the History of Gender and Empire, Comparative and Global Approaches*, (Bloomsbury Academic, 2018).

Eleanor Zeliot,[149] an American author and expert on the history of India, has famously said, 'One can hardly find a Marathi-speaking intellectual who did not speak out against untouchability, and one can find many who make it an important cause. But the institutions that carried out reforms were founded by non-Brahmins, and it may be said that this was an important enabling factor in the movements led by the untouchables themselves.'

Savitribai's willingness to take on the mighty Brahmins, at personal cost and peril, must be understood in the context of those times. Supported ably by Sagunabai to learn, she opened schools alongside Fatima Sheikh. But when she realized that she had to start awakening people's mindsets, so that more and more people would send their daughters to school, she started the Mahila Seva Mandal with Saraswati Govande and infanticide prevention homes with Jyotiba.

How have we allowed ourselves the impunity of forgetting these pioneers, on whose shoulders we stand?

The Last Meeting

After Fatima moved to Agra following her marriage to Barkat, she returned to Ahmednagar for the funeral of their beloved teacher Cynthia Fararr in 1862. When Savitri spotted Fatima, the latter looked divinely content, despite the fact that no one could escape a little sadness at the funeral of a beloved teacher.

She ran up to Fatima and hugged her.

Fatima had lost none of her disarming chatter. After pleasantries were exchanged, she said 'Can you believe, Aapa, that a woman travelled thousands of miles to come and spark a

149 Sabyasachi Bhattacharya, *Education and the Disprivileged: Nineteenth and Twentieth Century India*, (Orient Blackswan, 2002).

revolution? I wonder whether future generations will remember the kindness of Farrar madam.'

'History remembers kind people, Fatima. But I am upset with you. You write so well, yet you have never published anything. Maybe you should publish an essay about your experience with Farrar madam. At least we owe her that.'

'You are right, Aapa, we owe her that. But as Mohammed Paighambar has always said, *"Tum dharti waalon par daya karo, aakashwala tum par daya karega."* I am now teaching girls who have completed their basic education in madrasas and want to learn English and mathematics.'

'How I miss the evenings when you used to teach me about the great Prophet,' said Savitri nostalgically.

'Have I taught you anything at all, Aapa? It is your grace to say so!'

The two of them were then swarmed by several students, who were also delighted to see Fatima. There was a bond between them so strong that they stood together from the minute they saw each other at the funeral till the time that they left. And when they left, it was knowing that there would always be room in their hearts for each other and that no words would ever suffice or be needed.

Epilogue

Did Grace Summer and Usman get married? We do not know. Did Fatima Sheikh ever write letters to Savitribai Phule? We don't have any evidence to suggest this. What happened to Saraswati Govande? There is some reference that she joined the Sri Vicharvati Sabha in 1871,[150] whose aim was to propagate the eradication of caste discrimination. She continued to read the poems written by Savitribai Phule to gatherings of women, spreading the light.

What we do know is about the rest of Savitribai's venerated life till her death in 1897.

She remained undeterred by dissenters and continued her quest to liberate women and lower castes from the shackles of caste and patriarchy.

---

150 Dr Ganesh Raut

She continued with the same determined spirit because there was so much to be done. She edited and published Jyotirao Phule's speeches (25 December 1856). In 1863, the Phule couple started a home for pregnant widows so they could give birth to their children and live without the fear of ostracism.

As the backward classes were forbidden to drink water from the common village well, in 1868 Jyotirao and Savitribai dug a well in their own backyard and offered drinking water to all.

In 1873, the Phules established the Satyashodhak Samaj (Truth-seekers Society). Open to all people irrespective of caste and creed, the Satyashodhak movement launched a massive campaign against untouchability and superstition. Under this, the practice of the Satyashodhak marriage[151] further rejected Brahman-centric rituals and dowry and promoted inter-caste marriage.

Savitribai's selflessness was unimaginable. During the 1876-77 famine, she committed herself to providing relief and opened fifty-two free food hostels in Maharashtra.

In 1874, the Phule couple adopted Yashwantrao, the son of a widow Kashibai. The couple had sheltered Kashibai when conservative Brahmins in Poona had tried to kill her when she became a widow. Yashwantrao eventually became a doctor and married Radha in 1889. Radha's father was part of the social reform movement. An inter-caste marriage, it was performed with a simple garland exchange in defiance of being married traditionally by a Brahman pandit. The priestly class took offence to this marriage.

On 10 July 1887, Jyotirao made his will and had it registered at the office of the deputy registrar. In it, he noted with pride that Savitribai would take care of all the women in the various

151 A Satyashodhak marriage was a ceremony without priests and the usual religious rituals. This term was first coined by Mahatma Jyotirao Phule.

institutions run by them as if they were her own daughters. After Jyotirao Phule's death in 1890, Savitribai again challenged conventions and became the first woman in Indian history to light his pyre. Savitribai also took over as the chairperson of the Satyashodhak Samaj and carried forward Jyotirao's work.

Then came the famine of 1896, during which she once again worked extensively to provide relief to the affected families. Thereafter, in 1897, the bubonic plague spread across Maharashtra. Savitribai personally cared for the ill, as a result of which she contracted the disease. An anecdote mentions how Savitribai carried a ten-year-old boy from a Mahar settlement in Mundhwa to her adopted son Yashwantrao's clinic on the outskirts of Poona. Although the little boy survived, Savitribai caught the infection and succumbed to it on 10 March 1897 at the age of sixty-six.

Savitribai continues to be remembered as one of the most inspirational figures in the women's rights movement in India.

More than 200 books have been written on Jyotirao and Savitribai in Marathi. About forty of these have been written on Savitribai, including *Savitribai Jotirao Phule yanche Alpacharitra*, written by Shantabai Raghunath Bankar in 1939, and *Krantidevata Sadhvi Savitribai Phule*, written by Phulwantabai Zodage in 1966.

Following in their footsteps, Dr M.G. Mali wrote the biography *Krantijyoti Savitribai Jyotirao Phule* in 1980 and Dr K. P. Deshpande wrote *Agniphule* in 1982, based on Savitribai's life and literature.

The Government of India honoured her by publishing a postage stamp on 10 March 1998.

She is truly a priceless jewel of India and the world. We owe her.

Afterword

We will take the liberty to ascribe the afterword to the great Mahatma Jyotiba Phule. Here is a poem by him that sums up this book.

Vidyevina mati geli, mativina niti geli,
Nitivina gati geli, gativina vitta gele,
Vittavina shudra khachle, itke anarth avidyene kele.
(In the absence of knowledge, reason could not exist.
In the absence of reason, justice could not exist
In the absence of justice, progress could not exist
In the absence of progress, livelihood could not exist
In the absence of livelihood, the Shudras suffered.
All this disaster, due to the absence of knowledge.)

Facing page: Annexure 8 covers the import of Savitribai Phule's poems. This cover of *Kavyaphule* is reproduced with permission from Majestic Publications.

सावित्रीबाई फुले यांच्या 'काव्यफुले'
या काव्यसंग्रहावरील मुखपृष्ठ

ANNEXURES

These annexures have been crafted with zealous history students in mind. Those who want to go deeper into the story of Savitri and Fatima are at liberty to understand the context of the times in greater detail by reading the corresponding annexures, in line with the story. However, those who want a narrative feel might do well to read the story non-stop.

Annexure 1

Minute of Governor Sir Thomas Munro ordering the collection of detailed information on indigenous education.[152]

1. Much has been written both in England and in this country about the ignorance of the people of India and the means of disseminating knowledge among them. But the opinions upon this subject are the mere conjectures of individuals unsupported by any authentic documents and differing so widely from each other as to be entitled to very little attention.

Our power in this country and the nature of its own municipal institutions have certainly rendered it practicable

152 The full text of the minute of Governor Munro ordering a survey of indigenous education dated 25 June 1822 is in the Revenue Consultations, Vol. 920, dated 2 July 1822, available with Tamil Nadu State Archives, Chennai.

to collect material from which a judgment might be formed of the state of the mental cultivation of the people. We have made geographical and Agricultural surveys of our provinces. We have investigated their resources and endeavoured to ascertain their population, but little or nothing has been done to learn the state of education. We have no record to show the actual state of education throughout the country.

Partial inquiries have been made by individuals, but those have taken place at distant periods—and on a small scale and no inference can be drawn from them with regard to the country in general. There may be some difficulty in obtaining such a record as we want. Some districts will not—but others probably will furnish it—and if we get it only from two or three it will answer in some degree for all the rest. It cannot be expected to be very accurate, but it will at least enable us to form an estimate of the state of instructions among the people. The only record which can furnish the information required is a List of the schools in which reading and writing are taught in each district showing the number of scholars in each and the cast [sic] to which they belong. The Collectors should be directed to prepare this document according to the form which accompanies this paper. They should be desired to state the names of the books generally read at the schools.

The time which scholars usually continue at such schools. The monthly to yearly charge to the scholars and whether any of the schools are endowed by the Public and if so, the nature and the amount of the fund. When there are colleges or other institutions for teaching Theology, Law, Astronomy, etc. an account should be given of them. These sciences are usually taught privately without fee or reward by individuals to a few scholars or disciples, but there are also some instances in which the Native Governments have granted allowances in money and land for the maintenance of the Teachers.

2. In some districts, reading and writing are confined almost entirely to Bramins [sic] and the mercantile class. In some they extend to other classes and are pretty general among the Potails of villages and principal Royets. To the women of Bramins [sic] and of Hindoos in general they are unknown because the knowledge of them is prohibited and regarded as unbecoming of the modesty of the sex and fit only for public Dancers. But among the women of the Rujbundah and some other tribes of Hindoos who seem to have no prejudice of this kind, they are generally taught. The prohibition against women learning to read is probably from various causes, much less attended to in some Districts than in others and as it is possible that in every District a few females may be found in the reading schools, a column has been entered for them in the Form proposed to be sent to the Collector. The mixed and impure casts [sic] seldom learn to read, but as a few of them do, columns are left for them in the Form.

3. It is not my intention to recommend any interference whatever in the native schools. Everything of this kind ought to be carefully avoided, and the people should be left to manage their schools in their Own way. All that we ought to do is to facilitate the operations of these schools by restoring any funds that may have been diverted from them and perhaps granting additional ones, where it may appear advisable. But on this point we shall be better able to judge when we receive the information now proposed to be called for.

25 June 1822
Signed
Thomas Munro

Annexure 2

In 1835, the governor-general of India, Lord William Bentinck, commissioned William Adam to investigate the state of education in Bengal and Bihar and make recommendations for improvement. Adam turned in three reports (1835–1838). His study was a compilation of previous reports on the issue. This is an extract from Part 1. This is being reproduced here on account of its excellent detailing alone; the format of instruction followed by Persian schools or Arabic schools in the Agra Presidency, whichever kind Fatima and Usman Sheikh studied at, might be inferred from this.

Extract

Elementary Persian Schools (pp.148–152)

The Persian schools in Nattore are four in number, containing twenty-three scholars, who enter school at any age varying from four and a half to thirteen years, and leave it at an age varying from twelve to seventeen. The whole time stated to be spent at school varies from four to eight years. The teachers intellectually are of a higher grade than the teachers of Bengali schools, although that grade is not high compared with what is to be desired and is attainable. Morally, they appear to have as little notion as Bengali teachers of the salutary influence they might exercise on the dispositions and characters of their pupils.

They have no fees from the scholars and are paid in the form of fixed monthly allowances with perquisites. The monthly allowances vary from one rupee eight annas to four rupees, and they are paid by one, two or three families, who are the principal supporters of the school. The perquisites which are estimated at two rupees eight annas to six rupees a month and consist of food, washing and other personal expenses are provided either by the same parties or by those parents who do not contribute to the monthly allowance.

The total remuneration of the teacher varies from four to ten rupees per month, averaging at about seven rupees. The principal object of the patrons of these schools is the instruction of their own children; but in one instance, a worthy old Musalman, who has no children, contributes a small monthly allowance, without which the teacher would not have sufficient inducement to continue his labours; and in another case besides two children of the family, ten other boys are admitted, on whom instruction, food, and clothing are gratuitously bestowed. Two of the schools have separate school-houses [sic], which were built by the benevolent patrons who principally support them. The scholars of the other two assemble in out-buildings belonging to one or other of the families whose children receive instruction. Although in the Persian schools printed books are unknown, yet manuscript works are in constant use. The general course of instruction has no very marked stages or gradations into which it is divided.

Like the Hindoos, however, the Musalmans formally initiate their children into the study of letters. When a child, whether a boy or a girl, is four years, four months, and four days old, the friends of the family assemble, and the child is dressed in his best clothes, brought in to the company, and seated on a cushion in the presence of all. The alphabet, the form of letters used for computation, the introduction to the Koran, some verses of Chapter LV, and the whole of Chapter LXXXVII, are placed before him, and he is taught to pronounce them in succession. If the child is self-willed, and refuses to read, he is made to pronounce the Bismillah, which answers every purpose, and from that day his education is deemed to have commenced. At school he is taught the alphabet, as with ourselves, by the eye and ear, the forms of the letters being presented to him in writing and their names pronounced in his hearing, which he is required to repeat until he is able to connect the names and the forms with each other in his mind. The scholar is afterwards made to read the thirteenth section of the Koran, the chapters of which are short, and are generally used at the times of prayer and in the burial service. The words are marked with the diacritical points in order that the knowledge of letters, their junction and correct orthography and their pronunciation from the appropriate organs may be thoroughly acquired; but the sense is entirely unknown.

The next book put into his hands is the Pandanameh of Sadi, a collection of moral sayings, many of which are above his comprehension, but he is not taught or required to understand any of them. The work is solely used for the purpose of instructing him in the art of reading and of forming a correct pronunciation, without any regard to the sense of the words pronounced. It is generally after this that the scholar is taught to write the letters, to join vowels and consonants, and to form syllables. The next book is the Amadnameh, exhibiting the forms of conjugating the Persian verbs which are read to the master and by frequent repetition committed to memory.

The first book which is read for the purpose of being understood is the Gulistan of Sadi, containing lessons on life and manners and this is followed or accompanied by the Bostan of the same author. Two or three sections of each are read; and simultaneously short Persian sentences relating to going and coming, sitting and standing, and the common affairs of life, are read and explained. The pupil is afterwards made to write Persian names, then Arabic names and next Hindi names, especially such as contain letters to the writing or pronunciation of which difficulty is supposed to attach. Elegant penmanship is considered a great accomplishment, and those who devote themselves to this art employ from three to six hours every day in the exercise of it, writing first single letters, then double or treble, then couplets, quatrains etc. They first write upon a board with a thick pen, then with a finer pen on pieces of paper pasted together; and last of all, when they have acquired considerable command of the pen, they begin to write upon paper in single fold.

This is accompanied or followed by the perusal of some of the most popular poetical productions such as Joseph and Zuleikha, founded on a well-known incident in Hebrew history; the loves of Leila and Majnun; the Secandar Nameh, an account of the exploits of Alexander the Great, etc., etc. The mode of computing by the Abjad, or letters of the alphabet, is also taught, and is of two sorts; in the first, the letters of the alphabet in the order of the Abjad being taken to denote units, tens, and hundreds to a thousand; and in the second the letters composing the names of the letters of the alphabet being employed for the same purpose. Arithmetic, by means of the Arabic numerals, and instruction at great length in the different styles of address and in the forms of correspondence, petitions etc. complete a course of Persian instruction. In the Persian schools of the district, this course is very superficially taught and some of the teachers do not even profess to carry their pupils beyond the Gulistan and Bostan.

In a Persian school, after the years of mere childhood, when the pupils are assumed to be capable of stricter application, the hours of study with interval extend from six in the morning to nine at night. In the first place in the morning they revise the lessons of the previous day, after which a new lesson is read, committed to memory, and reported to the master. About mid-day they have leave of absence for an hour when they dine, and on their return to school they are instructed in writing. About three o'clock they have another reading lesson which is also committed to memory, and about an hour before the close of day they have leave to play. The practice with regard to the forenoon and afternoon lessons in reading, is to join the perusal of a work in prose with that of a work in verse; as the Gulistan with the Bostan and Abdulfazl's letters with the Secundar Nameh, the forenoon lesson being taken from one and the afternoon lesson from the other. In the evening they repeat the lessons of that day several times, until they have them perfectly at command; and, after making some preparation for the lessons of the next day, they have leave to retire. Thursday every week is devoted to the revision of old lessons; and when that is completed, the pupils seek instruction or amusement according to their own pleasure in the perusal of forms of prayer and stanzas of poetry, and are dismissed on that day at three o'clock without any new lesson.

On Friday, the sacred day of Musalmans, there is no schooling. In other districts in respectable or wealthy Musalman families, besides the literary instructor called Miyan or Akhun, there is also a domestic tutor or Censor Morum called Atalik, a kind of head-servant whose duty it is to train the children of the family to good manners, and to see that they do not neglect any duty assigned to them; but I do not find any trace of this practice in Rajshahy.

Upon the whole the course of Persian instruction, even in its less perfect forms such as are found to exist in this district, has a more comprehensive character and a more liberal tendency than that pursued in the Bengali schools. The systematic use of books although in manuscript is a great step in advance accustoming the minds of the pupils to forms of regular composition, to correct and elegant language and to trains of consecutive thought, and thus aiding both to stimulate the intellect and to form the taste. It might be supposed that the moral bearing of some of the text books would have a beneficial effect on the character of the pupils; but as far as I have been able to observe or ascertain, those books are employed like all the rest solely for the purpose of conveying lessons in language, lessons in the knowledge of sounds and words in the construction of sentences, or in anecdotal information, but not for the purpose of sharpening the moral perceptions or strengthening the moral habits.

This in general native estimation does not belong to the business of instruction, and it never appears to be thought of or attempted. Others will judge from their own observation and experience whether the Musalman character, as we see it in India, has been formed or influenced by such a course of instruction. The result of my own observations is that of two classes of persons, one exclusively educated in Mahomedan, and the other in Hindoo literature; the former appears to me to possess an intellectual superiority, but the moral superiority does not seem to exist.

Elementary Arabic Schools (pp.152–153)

The Arabic schools, or schools for instruction in the formal or ceremonial reading of certain passages of the Koran, are eleven in number, and contain 42 scholars, who begin to read at an age varying from 7 to 14, and leave school at an age varying from 8 to 18. The whole time stated to be spent at school varies from one to five years. The teachers possess the lowest degree of attainment to which it is possible to assign the task of instruction. They do not pretend to be able even to sign their names; and they disclaim altogether the ability to understand that which they read and teach. The mere forms, names, and sounds, of certain letters and combinations of letters they know and teach, and what they teach is all that they know of written language, without presuming, or pretending, or aiming to elicit the feeblest glimmering of meaning from these empty vocables. This whole class of schools is as consummate a burlesque upon mere forms of instruction, separate from a rational meaning and purpose, as can well be imagined.

The teachers are all Kath-Mollas, that is, the lowest grade of Musalman [sic] priests who chiefly derive their support from the ignorance and superstition of the poor classes of their co-religionists; and the scholars are in training for the same office. The portion of the Koran which is taught is that which begins with Chapter LXXVIII of Sale's Koran, and extends to the close of the volume. The Mollas, besides teaching a few pupils the formal reading of this portion of the Koran, perform the marriage ceremony, for which they are paid from one to eight annas according to the means of the party; and also the funeral service with prayers for the dead continued from one to forty days, for which they get from two annas to one rupee, and it is in these services that the formal reading of the Koran is deemed essential. The Mollas also often perform the office of the village butcher, killing animals for food with the usual religious forms, without which their flesh cannot be eaten by Musalmans [sic]; but for this they take no remuneration.

In several cases, the teacher of the school depends for his livelihood on employment at marriages and burials, giving his instructions as a teacher gratuitously. In one instance a fixed allowance is received from the patron of the school, fees from some of the scholars, and perquisites besides, amounting in all to four rupees eight annas per month, and in this case the patron professes the intention to have the scholars hereafter taught Persian and Bengali.

In another the patron merely lodges, feeds and clothes the teacher who receives neither fixed allowance nor fees. In three instances the only remuneration the teacher receives is a salami, or present of five or six rupees, from each scholar when he finally leaves school. In two instances the teachers have small farms from which they derive the means of subsistence in addition to their gains as Mollas. They give instruction either in their own houses, or in school-houses [sic], which are also applied to the purposes of prayer and hospitality and of assembly on occasions of general interest. No institutions can be more insignificant and useless, and in every respect less worthy of notice, than these Arabic schools, viewed as places of instruction; but, however worthless in themselves, they have a certain hold on the Native mind, which is proved by the increased respect and emoluments as Mollas, expected and acquired by some of the teachers on account of the instruction they give; the expense incurred by others of them in erecting school-houses [sic]; and by the general employment by the Musalman [sic] population of those who receive and communicate the slender education which these schools bestow.

In the eye of the philanthropist or the statesman no institution however humble, will be overlooked, by which he may hope beneficially to influence the condition of any portion of mankind; and it is just in proportion to the gross ignorance of the multitude that he will look with anxiety for any loop-holes [sic] by which he may find an entrance to their understandings—some institutions, which are held by them in veneration and which have hitherto served the cause of ignorance, but which he may hope with discretion to turn to the service of knowledge.

I do not despair that means might be employed, simple, cheap, and inoffensive, by which even the teachers of these schools might be reared to qualify themselves for communicating a much higher grade of instruction to a much greater number of learners without divesting them of any portion of the respect and attachment of which they are now the objects.

Annexure 3

Here is an extract from the book *Gulamgiri* (Slavery), written by Mahatma Jyotirao Phule. In the book, he talks about the crippling caste system in India, prevalent through the nineteenth century.

A Brahmin can do no wrong

Never shall the king slay a Brahmin, though he has committed all possible crimes.

To save the life of [a] Brahmin any falsehood may be told. There is no sin in it.

No one is to take away anything belonging to a Brahmin.

A king, though dying with want, must not receive any tax from a Brahmin, nor suffer him to be afflicted with hunger or the whole kingdom will be afflicted with famine.

The feet of [a] Brahmin are holy. In his left foot reside all the *tirtha* (holy waters at places of pilgrimage) and by dipping it into water he makes it as holy as the waters at the holiest of shrines.

A Brahmin may compel a man of the servile class to perform servile duty, because such a man was created by the almighty only for the purpose of serving Brahmins.

A Sudra, though emancipated by his master, is not released from [the] state of servitude; for being born in a state which is natural to him, by whom can he be divested of his natural attributes?

Let a Brahmin not give temporal advice nor spiritual counsel to a Sudra.

No superfluous accumulation of wealth shall be made by a Sudra, even though he has the power to make it, since a servile man who has amassed riches becomes proud, and by his insolence or neglect he gives pain even to Brahmins.

If a Sudra cohabit[s] with a Brahminee adulteress, his life is to be taken. But if a Brahmin goes even unto the lawful wife of a Sudra he is exempted from all corporal punishment.

My object in writing the present volume is not only to tell my Sudra brethren how they have been duped by the Brahmins, but also to open the eyes of Government to the pernicious system of high class education which has hitherto been so persistently followed and which statesmen like Sir George Campbell the present Lieutenant Governor of Bengal, with broad and universal sympathies, are finding to be highly mischievous and pernicious to the interests of Government.

I sincerely hope that Government will ere long see the error of their ways, trust less to writers or men who look through high class spectacles and take the glory into their own hands of emancipating my Sudra brethren from the trammels of bondage which the Brahmins have woven round them like the coils of a serpent. It is no less the duty of such of my Sudra brethren as have received any education to place before Government the true state of their fellow men and endeavour to the best of their power to emancipate themselves from Brahmin thraldom. Let there be [a] school for the Sudras in every village; but away with all Brahmin school-masters [sic]! The Sudras are the life and sinews of the country, and it is to them alone and to the Brahmins that the Government must ever look to tide them over their difficulties, financial as well as political. If the hearts and minds of the Shudras are made happy and contented the British Government need have no fear for their loyalty in the future.

Annexure 4

Below is a complete list of schools run by Jyotirao and Savitribai Phule, Fatima Sheikh and their associates.

Sr. No	Name of the school	Date of opening
1	Bhide Wada, Poona	1 January 1848
2	Mahar Wada, Poona	15 May 1848
3	Hadapsar, Poona	1 September 1848
4	Otur, Poona	5 December 1848
5	Saswad, Poona	20 December 1848
6	Alhatache-ghar, Poona	1 July 1849
7	Naigaon, Khandala, Satara	15 July 1849
8	Shirwal, Khandala, Satara	18 July 1849
9	Talegaon Dhamdhere, Poona	1 September 1849
10	Shirur, Poona	8 September 1849
11	Anjeer Wadi, Mazgaon	3 March 1850

Sr. No	Name of the school	Date of opening
12	Karanje, Satara	6 March 1850
13	Bhingar, Ahmednagar.	19 September 1850
14	Mundhwa, Poona	1 December 1850
15	Annasaheb Chiplunkar Wada, Poona	3 July 1851
16	Nana Peth, Poona	1 December 1851
17	Rast Peth, Poona	17 September 1851
18	Vetal Peth, Poona	15 March 1852

Annexure 5

Essay by Mukta Salve, female student of Fatima and Savitri's schools, titled 'Mang Maharachya Dukhvisayi':

It humbles me to realize that God has filled the heart of an untouchable girl like me, considered to be even lower than an animal, with the pain and suffering of my people—the Mahars and Mangs. The Creator of all beings has put this in my heart and while invoking His name, I dare to pen this essay with the strength I have now received.

The Creator is the one who created the Mangs, the Mahars and also the Brahmins and He is the one who is filling me with wisdom to write. He will bless my labour with a fruitful outcome. If we attempt to refute, on the basis of the Vedas, the argument of these gluttonous Brahmins, who hate us and consider themselves vastly superior, they say that the Vedas are their own domain, their exclusive property. Now apparently, if the Vedas are only for the Brahmins, they are obviously not for us. If the Vedas belong only to the Brahmins, then it is an open secret that we do not have the Book.

We are without the Book—we are without any religion. If the Vedas are for the Brahmins only, then we are not bound to act according to the Vedas. If merely looking at the Vedas can get us into grievous sins (as the Brahmins claim), then would not following them be the height of foolishness? Muslims lead their life according to their Koran, English people follow their Bible and Brahmins have their own Vedas. Because they all have their own good or bad religion that they follow, they are somewhat happier than us who are without any religion. Oh, God, please tell us, what is our religion? Teach us, O God, your true religion so that we all can lead our lives according to it.

Let that religion, where only one person is privileged and the rest deprived, vanish from the earth and let it never enter our minds to boast of such a [discriminatory] religion. These people drove us, the poor Mangs and Mahars, away from our own lands, which they occupied to build large buildings. And that was not all. They would make the Mangs and Mahars drink oil mixed with red lead and buried our people in the foundations of their buildings, thus wiping out generation after generation of our poor people. The Brahmans have degraded us so low; they consider people like us even lower than cows and buffaloes. Did they not consider us even lower than donkeys during the rule of Bajirao Peshwa? You beat a lame donkey, and his master retaliates.

But who was there to object to the routine thrashing of Mahars and Mangs? Under Bajirao's rule, if any Mang or Mahar happened to pass in front of a gymnasium, they would cut off his head and play 'bat and ball' with their swords as bats and his head as a ball, on the grounds. When we were punished for even passing through their doors, where was the question of getting education, getting freedom to learn? When any Mang or Mahar would learn somehow to read and write, and if Bajirao came to know about this, he would say: education of a Mang or Mahar amounts to taking away a Brahmin's job. He used to say, *'How dare they get educated? Do these untouchables expect the Brahmins to hand over their official duties to them and move around with their shaving kits, shaving the heads of widows?'* With such remarks he would punish them.

Secondly, were these Brahmins satisfied with prohibiting us from learning? Not at all. Bajirao went to Kashi and died an ignominious death there. But the Mahars here, no less untouchable than the Mangs, also avoid the company of the Mangs. They have acquired some Brahminical traits and consider themselves to be superior to the Mangs—they also get polluted by the shadow of Mangs! Do the stony hearted Brahmins, who proudly roam around in their so-called holy clothes to proclaim their superiority, ever feel even a frisson of compassion for us when we suffer so much on account of being labelled untouchables? Nobody gives us employment because we are untouchables. No job means no money. We have to endure grinding poverty.

O learned pundits, fold up your selfish priestcraft and stop the prattle of your hollow wisdom and listen to what I have to say. When our women give birth to babies, they do not have even a roof over their heads. How they suffer in the rain and the cold! Please try to understand it from your own experience. If they get some disease while giving birth, where will they get money for the doctor or medicines? Was there ever any doctor among you who was human enough to treat such people free of cost?

The Mang and Mahar children never dare lodge a complaint even if the Brahmin children throw stones at them and injure them seriously. They suffer silently because they know they have to go to the Brahmins' houses to beg for the leftover food. Alas! O God! What agony this! I will burst into tears if I write more about this injustice. Because of such oppression, the merciful God has bestowed on us, this benevolent British government. Let us see how our pain has been mitigated under this government. Earlier, Gokhale, Apate, Trimkaji, Andhala, Pansara, Kale, Behre, etc. [all Brahmin surnames], who showed their bravery by killing rats in their homes, persecuted us, not sparing even pregnant women, without any rhyme or reason. This has stopped now.

Harassment and torture of Mahars and Mangs, common during the rule of Peshwas in Poona, have stopped. Now, human sacrifice for the foundation of forts and mansions has stopped—now, nobody buries us alive. Now, our population is growing in numbers. Earlier, if any Mahar or Mang wore fine clothes, they would say that only Brahmins should wear such clothes. Seen in fine clothes, we were earlier accused of stealing such clothes. Their religion was in danger of being polluted when untouchables put clothes around their bodies; they would tie them to [a] tree and punish them. But, under British rule, anybody with money can buy and wear clothes. Earlier, punishment for any wrong-doing against the upper castes was to behead the guilty untouchable—now, it has stopped.

Excessive and exploitative tax has stopped. The practice of untouchability has stopped in some places. Killing has stopped on the playground. Now, we can even visit the marketplace. Under the impartial British rule, many such things have happened. As I write this, I am amazed that the Brahmins who earlier used to treat us like dirt, as I have written above, want to free us from our suffering. Not all the Brahmins though. Those who are influenced by Satan continue to hate us like before. They target and outcaste the Brahmins who are trying to liberate us. Some noble souls have started schools for Mahars and Mangs, and such schools are supported by the merciful British government. Oh, the Mahars and Mangs, you are poor and sick. Only the medicine of knowledge will cure and heal you. It will take you away from wild beliefs and superstitions. You will become righteous and moral. It will stop your exploitation.

People who treat you like animals will not dare to treat [you] like that any more. So please work hard and study. Get educated and become good human beings. But I cannot even prove this. For example, those who have received good education also sometimes surprise us by doing very bad deeds!

Mukta Salve

Annexure 6

Jyotirao Phule's deposition before the Education Commission in 1881 (also known as the Hunter Commission) is reproduced here from the book Selected Writings of Jyotirao Phule *(this extract is recorded between pages 140 and 145 in Education Commission, Bombay, Vol II, Calcutta, 1884).*

My experience in educational matters is principally confined to Poona and the surrounding villages. About 25 years ago, the missionaries had established a female school at Poona, but no indigenous school for girls existed at the time.

I, therefore, was induced, about the year 1851, to establish such a school, and in which I and my wife worked together for many years. After some time I placed this school under the management of a committee of educated natives. Under their auspices two more schools were opened in different parts of the town. A year after the institution of the female schools, I also established an indigenous mixed school for the lower classes, especially the Mahars and Mangs.

Two more schools for these classes were subsequently added, Sir Erskine Perry, the president of the late Educational Board, and Mr Lumsdain, the then Secretary to Government, visited the female schools and were much pleased with the movement set on foot, and presented me with a pair of shawls. I continued to work in them for nearly 9 to 10 years, but owing to circumstances, which it is needless here to detail, I seceded from the work.

These female schools still exist, having been made over by the committee to the Educational Department under the management of Mrs Mitchell. A school for the lower classes, Mahars and Mangs, also exists at the present day, but not in a satisfactory condition. I have also been a teacher for some years in a mission female boarding school. My principal experience was gained in connection with these schools. I devoted some attention also to the primary education available in this Presidency and have had some opportunities of forming an opinion as to the system and personnel employed in the lower schools of the Educational Department. I wrote some years ago a Marathi pamphlet exposing the religious practices of the Brahmins and incidentally among other matters, adverted therein to the present: system of education, which by providing ampler funds for higher education tended to educate Brahmins and the higher classes only, and to leave the masses wallowing in ignorance and poverty. I summarised the views expressed in the book in an English preface attached thereto, portions of which I reproduce here so far as they relate to the present enquiry:

> Perhaps a part of the blame in bringing matters to this crisis may be justly laid to the credit of the Government. Whatever may have been their motives in providing ampler funds and greater facilities for higher education,

and neglecting that of the masses, it will be acknowledged by all that injustice to the latter, this is not as it should be. It is an admitted fact that the greater portion of the revenues of the Indian Empire are derived from the ryot's labour from the sweat of his brow. The higher and richer classes contribute little or nothing to the state exchequer. A well-informed English writer states that our income is derived, not from surplus profits, but from capital; not from luxuries, but from the poorest necessaries. It is the product of sin and tears.

That Government should expend profusely a large portion of revenue thus raised, on the education of the higher classes, for it is these only who take advantage of it, is anything but just or equitable. Their object in patronising this actual high class education appears to be to prepare scholars who, it is thought would in time vend learning without money and without price. If we can inspire, say they, the love of knowledge in the minds of the superior classes, the result will be a higher standard of morals in the cases of the individuals, a large amount of affection for the British Government, and unconquerable desire to spread among their own countrymen the intellectual blessings which they have received.

Regarding these objects of Government the writer above alluded to, states that we have never heard of [a] philosophy more benevolent and more utopian. It is proposed by men who witness the wondrous changes brought about in the Western world purely by the agency of popular knowledge, to redress the defects of the two hundred millions of India by giving superior education to the superior classes and to them only. We ask the friends of Indian Universities to favour us with a single example of the truth of their theory from the instances which have already fallen within the scope of their experience. They have educated many children of wealthy men and have been the means of advancing very materially the worldly prospects of some of their pupils. But what contribution have these made to great work of regenerating their fellow men? How have they begun to act upon the masses? Have any of them formed classes at their own homes or elsewhere, for the instruction of their less fortunate or less wise countrymen? Or have they kept their knowledge to themselves, as a personal gift, not to be soiled by contact with the ignorant vulgar? Have they in any way shown themselves anxious to advance the general interests and repay the philanthropy with patriotism? Upon what grounds is it asserted that the best way to advance the moral and intellectual welfare of the people is to raise the standard of instruction among the higher classes? A glorious argument this for aristocracy, were it only tenable. To show the growth of the national happiness, it would only be necessary to refer to the number of pupils at the colleges and the lists of academic degrees. Each wrangler would be accounted a national benefactor; and the existence of Deans and Proctors would be associated, like the game laws and the ten-pound franchise, with the best interests of the constitution.

One of the most glaring tendencies of [the] Government system of high class education has been the virtual monopoly of all the higher offices under them by Brahmins. If the welfare of the Ryot is at heart, if it is the duty of Government to check a host of abuses, it behoves them to narrow this monopoly day by day so as to allow a sprinkling of the other castes to get into the public services. Perhaps some might be inclined to say that it is not feasible in the present state of education. Our only reply is that if Government look a little less after higher education which is able to take care of itself and more towards the education of the masses there would be no difficulty in training up a body of men every way qualified and perhaps far better in morals and manners.

My object in writing the present volume is not only to tell my Shudra brethren how they have been duped by the Brahmins, but also to open the eyes of Government to that pernicious system of high class education, which has hitherto been so persistently followed, and which statesmen like Sir George Campbell, the present Lieutenant Governor of Bengal, with broad universal sympathies, are finding to be highly mischievous and pernicious to the interests of Government. I sincerely hope that Government will ere long see the error of their ways, trust less to writers or men who look through high class spectacles, and take the glory into their own hands of emancipating my Shudra brethren from the trammels of bondage which the Brahmins have woven around them like the coils of a serpent. It is no less the duty of each of my Shudra brethren as have received any education, to place before Government the true state of their fellow men and endeavour to the best of their power to emancipate themselves from Brahmin thraldom. Let there be schools for the Shudras in every village; but away with all Brahmin school-masters [sic]! The Shudras are the life and sinews of the country, and it is to them alone, and not to the Brahmins, that Government must ever look to tide over their difficulties, financial as well as political. If the hearts and minds of the Shudras are made happy and content, the British Government need have no fear for their loyalty in the future.

Primary Education

There is little doubt that primary education among the masses in this presidency has been very much neglected. Although the number of primary schools now in existence is greater than those existing a few years ago, yet they are not commensurate to the requirements of the community. Government collects a special cess for educational purposes, and it is to be regretted that this fund is not spent for the purposes for which it is collected. Nearly nine-tenths of the villages in this presidency, or nearly 10 lakhs of children, it is said, are without any provisión, whatever, for primary instruction. A good deal of their poverty, their want of self-reliance, their entire dependence upon the learned and intelligent classes, is attributable to this deplorable state of education among the peasantry.

Even in towns the Brahmins, the Purbhoos, the hereditary classes, who generally live by the occupation of pen, and the trading classes seek primary instruction. The cultivating and the other classes, as a rule, do not generally avail themselves of the same. A few of the latter class are found in primary and secondary schools, but owing to their poverty and other causes they do not continue long at school. As there are no special inducements for these to continue at school, they naturally leave off as soon as they find menial or other occupation. In villages also most of the cultivating classes hold aloof owing to extreme poverty, and also because they require their children to tend cattle and look after their fields. Besides an increase in the number of schools, special inducements in the shape of scholarships and half-yearly or annual prizes to encourage them to send their children to school and thus create in them a taste for learning is most essential. I think primary education of the masses should be made compulsory up to a certain age, say at least 12 years. Muhammadans also hold aloof from these schools, as they somehow evince no liking for Marathi or English. There are a few Muhammadan primary schools where their own language is taught. The Mahars, Mangs, and other lower classes are practically excluded from all schools owing to caste prejudices, as they are not allowed to sit by the children of higher castes. Consequently special schools for these have been opened by Government. But these exist only in large towns. In the whole of Poona and for a population exceeding over 5000 people, there is only one school and in which the attendance is under 30 boys. This state of matters is not at all creditable to the educational authorities. Under the promise of the Queen's Proclamation I beg to urge that Mahars, Mangs, and other lower classes, where their number is large enough, should have separate schools for them, as they are not allowed to attend the other schools owing to caste prejudices.

In the present state of education, payment by results is not at all suitable for the promotion of education amongst a poor and ignorant people, as no taste has yet been created among them for education. I do not think any teacher would undertake to open schools on his own account among these people, as he would not be able to make a living by it. Government schools and special inducements, as noted above, are essential until such a taste is created among them.

With regard to the few Government primary schools that exist in the Presidency, I beg to observe that the primary education imparted in them is not at all placed on a satisfactory or sound basis. The system is imperfect insofar as it does not prove practical and useful in the future career of the pupils. The system is capable of being developed up to the requirement of the community if improvements that will result in its future usefulness be effected in it. Both the teaching machinery employed and the course in instruction now followed require a thorough remodelling.

(a) The teachers now employed in the primary schools are almost all Brahmins; a few of them are from the normal training college, the rest being all untrained men. Their salaries are very low, seldom exceeding Rs. 10, and their attainments also very meagre. But as a rule they are all unpractical men, and the boys who learn under them generally imbibe inactive habits and try to obtain service, to the avoidance of their hereditary or other hardy or independent professions. I think teachers for primary schools should be trained, as far as possible, out of the cultivating classes, who will be able to mix freely with them and understand their wants and wishes much better than a Brahmin teacher who generally holds himself aloof under religious prejudices. These would moreover exercise a more beneficial influence over the masses than teachers of other classes and who will not feel ashamed to hold the handle of a plough or the carpenter's adze when required, and who will be able to mix themselves readily with the lower orders of society. The course of training for them ought to include, besides the ordinary subjects, elementary knowledge of agriculture and sanitation. The untrained teachers should, except when thoroughly efficient, be replaced by efficient trained teachers. To secure a better class of teachers and to improve their position, better salaries should be given. Their salaries should not be less than Rs. 12 and in larger villages should be at least Rs. 15 or 20. Associating them in the village polity as auditors of village accounts or registrars of deeds, or village postmasters or stamp vendors would improve their status, and thus exert a beneficial influence over the people along whom they live. The school masters of village schools who pass a large number of boys should also get some special allowance other than their pay, as an encouragement to them.

(b) The course of instruction should consist of reading, writing Modi and Balbodh and accounts, and a rudimentary knowledge of general history, general geography, and grammar, also an elementary knowledge of agriculture and a few lessons on moral duties and sanitation. The studies in the village schools might be fewer than those in larger villages and towns, but not less practical. In connection with lessons in agriculture, a small model farm, where practical instruction to the pupils can be given, would be a decided advantage and, if really efficiently managed, would be productive of the greatest good to the country. The text-books [sic] in use, both in the primary and Anglo-vernacular schools, require revision and recasting as much as they are not practical or progressive in their scope. Lessons on technical education and morality, sanitation and agriculture, and some useful arts should be interspersed among them in progressive series. The fees in the primary schools should be as 1 to 2[153] [sic] from the children of cess-payers and non-cess payers.

(c) The supervising agency over these primary schools is also very defective and insufficient. The Deputy Inspector's visit once a year can hardly be of any appreciable benefit. All these schools ought at least to be inspected quarterly if not oftener. I would also suggest the advisability of visiting these schools at other times and without any intimation being given. No reliance can be placed on the district or village officers owing to the multifarious duties devolving on them, as they seldom find time to visit them, and when they do, their examination is necessarily very superficial and imperfect. European Inspector's supervision is also occasionally very desirable, as it will tend to exercise a very efficient control over the teachers generally.

153 This appears to be a ratio.

(d) The number of primary schools should be increased—

1. By utilising such of the indigenous schools as shall be or are conducted by trained and certificated teachers, by giving them liberal grants-in-aid.
2. By making over one half of the local cess fund for primary education alone.
3. By compelling, under a statutory enactment, municipalities to maintain all the primary schools within their respective limits.
4. By an adequate grant from the provincial or imperial funds.

Prizes and scholarships to pupils, and capitation or other allowances to the teachers, as an encouragement, will tend to render these schools more efficient.

The Municipalities in large towns should be asked to contribute whole share of the expenses incurred on primary schools within the municipal area. But in no case ought the management of the same to be entirely made over to them. They should be under the supervision of the Educational Department.

The Municipalities should also give grants-in-aid to such secondary and private English schools as shall be conducted according to the rules of the Educational Department, where their funds permit, such grants-in-aid being regulated by the number of boys passed every year. These contributions from municipal funds may be made compulsory by statutory enactment.

The administration of the funds for primary education should ordinarily be in the hands of the Director of Public Instruction.

But if educated and intelligent men are appointed on the local or district committees, these funds may be safely entrusted to them, under the guidance of the Collector, or the Director of Public Instruction. At present, the local boards consist of ignorant and uneducated men, such as Patels, Inamdars, Surdars,

& C. who would not be capable of exercising any intelligent control over the funds.

Indigenous Schools

Indigenous schools exist a good deal in cities, towns and some large villages, especially where there is a Brahmin population. From the latest reports of Public Instruction in this presidency, it is found that there are 1,049 indigenous schools with about 27,694 pupils in them. They are conducted on the old village system. The boys are generally taught the multiplication table by heart, a little Modi writing and reading, and to recite a few religious pieces. The teachers, as a rule, are not capable of effecting any improvements, as they are not initiated in the art of teaching. The fees charged in these schools range from 2 to 8 annas. The teachers generally come from the dregs of Brahminical society. Their qualifications hardly go beyond reading and writing Marathi very indifferently, and casting accounts up to the rule of three or so. They set up as teachers as the last resource of getting a livelihood. Their failure or unfitness in other callings of life obliges them to open schools. No arrangements exist in the country to train up teachers for indigenous schools. The indigenous schools could not be turned to any good account, unless the present teachers are replaced by men from the training colleges and by those who pass the 6th standard in the vernaculars. The present teachers will willingly accept State aid but money thus spent will be thrown away. I do not know any instance in which a grant-in-aid is paid to such a school. If it is being paid anywhere, it must be in very rare cases. In my opinion no grants-in-aid should be paid to such schools unless the master is a certificated one. But if certificated or competent teachers be found, grant-in-aid should be given and will be productive of great good.

Higher Education

The cry over the whole country has been for some time past that Government has amply provided for higher education, whereas that of the masses has been neglected. To some extent this cry is justified, although the classes directly benefitted by the higher education may not readily admit it. But for all this no well-wisher of his country would desire that Government should, at the present time, withdraw its aid from higher education. All that they would wish is, that as one class of the body politic has been neglected, its advancement should form as anxious a concern as that of the other. Education in India is still in its infancy. Any withdrawal of State aid from higher education cannot but be injurious to the spread of education generally.

A taste for education among the higher and wealthy classes, such as the Brahmins and Purbhoos, especially those classes who live by the pen, has been created, and a gradual withdrawal of State aid may be possible so far as these classes are concerned; but in the middle and lower classes, among whom higher education has made no perceptible progress, such a withdrawal would be a great hardship. In the event of such withdrawal, boys will be obliged to have recourse to inefficient and sectarian schools much against their wish, and the cause of education cannot but suffer. Nor could any part of such education be entrusted to private agency. For a long time to come the entire educational machinery, both ministerial and executive, must be in the hands of Government. Both the higher and primary education require all the fostering care and attention which Government can bestow on it.

The withdrawal of Government from schools or colleges would not only tend to check the spread of education, but would seriously endanger that spirit of neutrality which has all along been the aim of Government to foster, owing to the different nationalities and religious creeds prevalent in India. This withdrawal may, to a certain extent, create a spirit of self-reliance for local purposes in the higher and wealthy classes, but the cause of education would be so far injured that the spirit of self-reliance would take years to remedy that evil. Educated men of ability, who do not succeed in getting into public service, may be induced to open schools for higher education on being assured of liberal grants-in-aid. But no one would be ready to do so on his own account as a means of gaining a livelihood, and it is doubtful whether such private efforts could be permanent or stable, nor would they succeed half so well in their results. Private schools such as those of Mr. Vishnu Shastree Chiploonkar and Mr. Bhavey exist in Poona, and with adequate grants-in-aid may be rendered very efficient, but they can never supersede the necessity of the high school.

The Missionary schools, although some of them are very efficiently conducted, do not succeed half so well in their results, nor do they attract half the number of students which the high school attract. The superiority of Government schools is mainly owing to the richly paid staff of teachers and professors which it is not possible for a private school to maintain.

The character of instruction given in the Government higher schools is not at all practical, or such as is required for the necessities of ordinary life. It is only good to turn out so many clerks and schoolmasters. The Matriculation examination unduly engrosses the attention of the teachers and pupils, and the course of studies prescribed has no practical element in it, so as to fit the pupil for his future career in independent life. Although the number of students presenting for the Entrance examination is not at all large when the diffusion of knowledge in the country is taken into consideration, it looks large when the requirements of Government service are concerned. Were the education universal and within easy reach of all, the number would have been larger still, and it should be so, and I hope it will be so hereafter. The higher education should be so arranged as to be within easy reach of all, and the books on the subjects for the Matriculation examination should be published in the Government Gazette, as is done in Madras and Bengal. Such a course will encourage private studies and secure larger diffusion of knowledge in the country. It is a boon to the people that the Bombay University recognises private studies in the case of those presenting for the entrance examination. I hope the University authorities will be pleased to extend the same boon to higher examinations. If private studies were recognized by the University in granting the degrees of B.A., M.A. &c., many young men will devote their time to private studies. Their doing so will still further tend to the diffusion of knowledge. It is found in many instances quite impossible to prosecute studies at the colleges for various reasons. If private studies be recognised by the University, much good will [be] effected to the country at large, and a good deal of the drain on the public purse on account of higher education will be lessened.

The system of Government scholarships, at present followed in the Government schools, is also defective, as much as it gives undue encouragement to those classes only, who have already acquired a taste for education to the detriment of the other classes. The system might be so arranged that some of these scholarships should be awarded to such classes amongst whom education has made no progress.

The system of awarding them by competition, although abstractedly equitable, does not tend to the spread of education among other classes.

With regard to the question as to educated natives finding remunerative employments, it will be remembered that the educated natives who mostly belong to the Brahminical and other higher classes are mostly fond of service. But as the public service can afford no field for all the educated natives who come out from schools and colleges, and moreover the course of training they receive being not of a technical or practical nature, they find great difficulty in betaking themselves to other manual or remunerative employment. Hence the cry that the market is overstocked with educated natives who do not find any remunerative employment. It may, to a certain extent, be true that some of the professions are overstocked, but this does not show that there is no other remunerative employment to which they can betake themselves. The present number of educated men is very small in relation to the country at large, and we trust that the day may not be far distant when we shall have the present number multiplied a hundred-fold and all betaking themselves to useful and remunerative occupations and not be looking after service.

In conclusion, I beg to request the Education Commission to be kind enough to sanction measures for the spread of female primary education on a more liberal scale.

Poona,

19 October 1882.

Joteerao Govindrao Phooley,
Merchant and Cultivator and
Municipal Commissioner,
Peth Joona Ganja.

Annexure 7

Below is a letter written from Naigon Peth, when Savitri had gone to visit her parents at a time when she was unwell. This is the single most important historical reference to Fatima Sheikh.[154]

10 October 1856

Satya Swaroop Jyotirao Phule

Savitri salutes you!

After many fluctuations, it seems my health has been fully restored. My brother has served and nursed me with great devotion through my sickness. I got a glimpse of how loving he really is! I want to regain all my strength before I make the

154 Translated by the author from Dr M.G. Mali, *Krantijyoti Savitribai Jyotirao Phule*, (Majestic Publishing House, 1980).

trip to Poona. Please do not worry about me. I know my absence causes Fatima so much trouble. We are blessed that she is not the kind to grumble.

As we were talking one day, my brother said, 'You and your husband have rightly been expelled by your own community because both of you serve the untouchables (Mahars and Mangs). The untouchables are fallen people and by helping them you are bringing a bad name to our family. That is why I tell you to behave according to the customs of our caste and obey the dictates of the Brahmins.'

Mother was so disturbed by this uncontrolled rant by my brother.

Though my brother is a good soul he is extremely parochial; so he did not hesitate to bitterly criticize and reproach us. My mother, being the kind soul she is, did not reprimand him but tried instead to bring him to his senses, 'God has given you a kind countenance and a beautiful tongue, don't misuse it so!' I thought that mother's words made him feel ashamed of what he had just said. So he sat quietly. However, I wanted to oppose his point of view strongly. I defended our social work and tried to dispel his misgivings. I told him, 'Brother, your mind is narrow, and the Brahmins' teaching has made it worse. Animals like goats and cows are not untouchable for you, you lovingly touch them. You catch poisonous snakes on the day of the snake festival and feed them milk. But you consider Mahars and Mangs, who are as human as you and I, untouchables. Can you give me any reason for this? When the Brahmins perform their religious duties in their holy clothes, they consider you also impure and untouchable, they are afraid that your touch will pollute them. They don't treat you differently than the Mahars.'

When my brother heard this, he turned red in the face. He was even more aggressive this time, 'Why do you teach those

Mahars and Mangs? People abuse you because you teach the untouchables. I cannot bear it when people abuse and create trouble for you for doing that. I cannot tolerate such insults.'

I told him about what the English folk were doing for the Mahars and Mangs by offering to teach them; because being ignorant is like being an animal. When he acquires knowledge, he loses his lower status and achieves the higher one. This is what the Brahmins don't want, so obviously they are going to speak badly about us. My husband is a god-like man. He is beyond comparison in this world, nobody can equal him. He thinks the Untouchables must learn and attain freedom. He confronts the Brahmins and fights with them to ensure Teaching and Learning for the Untouchables because he believes that they are human beings like others and they should live as dignified humans. For this they must be educated. I also teach them for the same reason. What is wrong with that? Yes, we both teach girls, women, Mangs and Mahars. The Brahmins are upset because they believe this will upset their 'reign of fear'. That is why they oppose us and call our work 'Abrahminya, Abramhaya' or against Dharma. See, they have succeeded in poisoning the mind of a kind and caring person like you!

'You surely remember that the British Government had organised a function to honour my husband for his great work. His felicitation caused these vile people much heartburn. Let me tell you that my husband does not merely invoke God's name and passively claim to be interested in people's welfare. He is doing God's own work. And I assist him in that. I enjoy doing this work. I get immeasurable joy by doing such service. It is only now that I realise how limitless human capacity is.'

My mother and brother were listening intently. My brother finally came around, repented for what he had said and asked for forgiveness. Mother said, 'I think Goddess Saraswati resides inside you, Savitri. I am blessed and liberated by your thoughts and your words.'

The acknowledgement and appreciation from my mother and brother gladdened my heart. Now, if I went through this in my own house, you can imagine that there are many clowns here, as in Poona, who poison people's minds and spread canards against us. But why should we fear them and leave our purpose? The best use of our time would be to dive even more wholeheartedly into our work. Success will be ours in the future. The future belongs to us.

What more could I write?

With humble regards,

Yours,
Savitri

Annexure 8

A study of Savitri Phule's poetry shows the kind of person she was—well-rounded, liberated and balanced.

According to an estimate by renowned essayist Dr K.P. Deshpande,[155] Savitri Phule must have started writing poetry around 1850. However, it is important to note that her poems were written at least thirty years before those of Keshavasuta,[156] who is widely considered the first Marathi poet. So what does that make Savitri? There does not seem to be another published

155 Prof. Hari Narke (ed.), *Mahatma Phule, Sahitya Ani Chalval*, (Mahatma Jyotirao Phule Charitre Sadhane Prakashan Samiti, Maharashtra Government, 2006).

156 Krishnaji Keshav Damle (nickname: Keshavsut) (7 October 1866–7 November 1905) was a Marathi poet. Santakavya and Pantakavya were traditions in Marathi. Keshavsut, who broke these and wrote poems on other subjects, is considered the first Marathi poet.

Marathi poet at the time and even if there was, those records have not been preserved.

The question that faces a reader of Savitri's poems is whether she was a talented poet. Did she construct poems in her head even as a child, roaming in her father's garden? Did she want to study so that she could write poetry? Or did she write purely as service—to further the cause of social upliftment? You, the reader, will have to make your own decision, even as I propose a possible theory.

Savitribai Phule's first book, *Kavya Phule*, was brought out by Sheela Press in 1844. It comprises forty-one poems that can be broadly divided into seven themes, namely, nature, social issues, prayers, autobiographical, poetic, instructive and historical.

Let us consider the poem titled 'Drishta Kavi'.

Sarovar Manas Suvasik Phulanche
Tithe Bandhito Mahaal Kamlache
Char Vidyechi Chausasht Kalanchi
Subak Navratne Tyavar Rasachi
Kadhi Kalpi Mi Vishwa Mitra Aahe
Kavya Majhe He Pratisrushti Aahe.

(A poet is a person blessed by the divine. With the sacred fragrance of flowers, the palace dreams of building a palace with lotuses. The goddess resides in the poet's heart and it is only because of the divine blessing of knowledge and the arts that the poet is able to write. The classic treasure of the navarasas, the nine gems that define a range of emotions, are at the disposal of this poet. Hence, the poet is a friend of the world and poetry emerges from within them as a natural instinct.)

In 'Majhi Janmabhoomi', Savitri pays homage to her birthplace.

Bara Baluti Bara Aluti,Kitik Jaati Jamati
Shivarat Ya Sukhe Nandti
Paoospaani Chhan Padatase, Yeti Pike Saari
Vihirivar Phale Phule Gojiri
Gulzar Pakshi Gaati Manohar Fulpankhare
Aisa Nisarga Tithe Vavare
Baliraja Thor Hoi Shektari Daanshur
Janu Majhi Janmabhoomi Baliche Kashyappur II
(So many hereditary professions, religions and castes coexist in my beautiful village. Blessed with plentiful rainfall and flourishing crops that feed them, there is happiness all around. The place where I was born is characterized by overflowing wells, a cornucopia of flowers and sweet fruits. Birds and butterflies hover around the roses in the garden and sing melodious songs. Our people are strong, our farmers are courageous, generous and intelligent like King Baliraja. I am in gratitude to my homeland.)

The poem 'Maanav Va Praani' shows that her thinking was nuanced and refined:

Sundar Srishti Sundar Manav Sundar Jivan Saare
Sadbhavachya Parjanyane Bahroon Taku Vaare
Manav Jeevan He Viksuya
Bhay Chinta Saari Soduniya
Itra Jagvu Svataha Jaguya.
(The world is a beautiful place, let the winds of goodwill precipitate. Let us spread progress, overcome fear and worry. Awaken others and ourselves too.)

She also wrote a poem, 'Ingraji Shika', about the need to study English.

Vidyevin gele vaya gele pashu
Svasta Naka Basu, Vidya Ghene
Shudra Atishudra Dukh Nivaraya
Ingraji Shikaya Sandhi Aali
Ingraji Shikun Jaatibhed Moda
Bhatji Bharuda Fekuniya.
(Alas, animals cannot learn! But you can, so don't be lazy. Get knowledge and let us take the sadness of Shudras, Atishudras away. Here's your chance to learn English and understand that there is no caste system in the rest of the world. So we can break it. Let us overthrow the crushing weight of these Brahmins.)

She wrote a lot about the advice she would like to give society in poems such as 'Shresthadhan' and 'Balaas Updeshi'. One of her most well-known poems is a critique on who deserves to be called human.

Tayas Maanav Mhanave Ka?
(Do they deserve to be called human?)

Gyan Naahi, Vidya Naahi
Te Gheneche Godi Naahi
Buddhi Asuni Chaalat Nahi
Tayas Maanav Mhanave Ka?
(Those who have no knowledge
Nor desire to seek it
And do not apply their minds
Do they deserve to be called human?)

De Re Hari Palangi Kaahi
Pashuhi Aise Bolat Nahi
Vochar Na Aachar Nahi
Tayas Maanav Mhanave Ka?
(Those who treat humans
worse than animals;
and have no remorse either
Do they deserve to be called human?)

Porey Gharat Kami Nahit
Tayanchya Khanyasathihi
Na Kari To Udyog Kahi
Tayas Maanav Mhanave Ka?
(Those who have dependent children
And yet don't feed them
Or work towards it
Do they deserve to be called human?)

Sahanubhooti Milat Nahi
Madat Na Mile Konachihi
Parva Na Kari Kashachihi
Tayas Manav Mhanave Ka?
(Those who receive no compassion
Nor help
Neither do they care
Do they deserve to be called human?)

Dusryat Madat Naahi
Seva Tyag Daya Maya Nahi
Jayapashi Sadgun Naahi
Tayas Manav Mhanave Ka?

(Those who help no one
And have no empathy
Nor good habits
Do they deserve to be called human?)

Jyotish Ramal Saamudrikahi
Swarga Narkachya Kalpanahi
Pashut Nahi Tya Jo Pahi
Tayas Manav Mhanave Ka?
(Living a life of superstition
With idle thoughts of heaven and hell
Unconnected to reality
Do they deserve to be called human?)

Baeel Kaam Karit Rahi
Aitoba Ha Khaat Rahi
Pashu Pakshat Aise Nahi
Tayas Manav Mhanave Ka?
(The wife works all day
The man keeps eating his way
Such unique specimens
Do they deserve to be called human?)

Pashu Pakshi Makad Manus-hi
Janma Mrutyu Sarvanahi
Yache Gyan Jarahi Nahi
Tayas Manav Mhanave Ka?
(We are all mortal, fleeting
Animals, birds, monkeys all
Those who know this not
Do they deserve to be called human?)

She has also written devotional poems such as 'Shiva Prarthana', 'Shiva Stotra' and one on Maharani Tarabai titled 'Rani Chhatrapati Tarabai'.

Shatruvar Ghali Chapa, Kaal Tayachi Tee Hoyi
Jeris Shatrula Karuni Kari, Befami Chadhayi
Nhauni Taki Ranbhoomi
Shatru Raktani Saari.
Chapalta Vijechi Jaisi
Tasheech Kadade Saunhari
Hi Ekach Shoor Rangaani Chattrapati Tarabai.
(A terror to her enemies,
Making them helpless with unrestrained warfare
The battlefield
Is wet with the enemy's blood
Her quick victory
Caused by absolute destruction
Such a brave warrior, Rani Chhatrapati Tarabai.)

There is some conjecture on how well-read Savitri was. Her poems indicate that she likely did read a lot. Not only did she write on religious texts and Puranas, but she also used words such as 'native' and 'Indian' in her poems, indicating a comfortable familiarity with the English language.

During the famine of 1876–77, she was livid with the social situation and wrote a few scathing stanzas against the Brahmins, as follows:

Nahi Paoos Padla Kothehi
Mhanoon Peek Pani Kahi Nahi
Yaney Hoti Dushkalahi
Kop Nasey Devacha

Dushkal Hi Papachi Gati
Shudradi Atishudra Bhogati
Chamchamit Khaoon Vadati
Punyatle Punyavan II
(Not a drop of rainfall,
No water to drink
This famine
Is not the wrath of Gods,
But the outcome of sins
Shudras and Atishudras suffer,
While a feast is served
To the Brahmin Pundits of Poona!)

The above lines are a testimony to the fact that during the famine, the state of the people was pitiable; they would do anything for a plate of food. Starved of compassion and dignity, they were vulnerable. Savitri identified this abject helplessness as the reason why people underwent religious conversion. Hers was clearly a fearless mind that voiced what she observed. Even though she never endorsed religious conversion, she understood why people opted for it and wrote a powerful four-line stanza, as follows.

Nana Katha Chitra Vichitre, Davti Khoti Puran Sutre,
Dharma Karmachi Bhaychitre, Sarvanpudhe Karuniya
Yala Kantaloon Jan Jaati, Vaitagoon Khristi Hoti,
Muslaman Dharma Svikarti, Hey Paap Kunache II
(Elaborate stories and paintings, false interpretations,
Fear-mongering via religion, is the work of Brahmins.
The people are tired of their own Dharma
And converting to Christianity and Islam
Who is responsible?)

In essence, these poems written by Savitri Phule are probably our best means of understanding her character.

And what do they tell us? Here is what I would like to suggest as a possible interpretation. Savitribai Phule was far ahead of her times. She could certainly be called an active feminist and social reformer because she stepped forward to act on the problems that she saw. She also wrote poems in praise of Jyotirao. She was a devoted wife and her devotion rested on respect. In terms of style, sometimes she wrote with an assertive directness and at other times she wrote with fluid ease. There is a thread of descriptive imagination that brings her poetry alive.

To my mind, she was a gifted poet who wrote for herself as well as for others. She was fired by purpose and an appreciation of human values.

Annexure 9

How do we know so many of the instances woven into our story? The power of the intellectuals of the time, who were passionate about documentation, cannot be underestimated. There was an unprecedented mushrooming of journals and news papers in the nineteenth century. Journalism was decidedly the most effective mode of dissemination of reform ideas and initiatives during the period. At the beginning of 1880 there were approximately seventy-seven Indian-owned newspapers in Bombay Presidency with a total circulation of 30,600, thus giving an effective readership of about three lakhs. By the end of 1885 the number of Indian-owned papers in the Presidency rose to 133 with a total circulation of 62,729 and an effective readership of over six lakhs.[157]

157 Hulas Singh, *Rise of Reason: Intellectual History of 19th-century Maharashtra*, (Routledge, 2015).

Here are a few important newspapers and editors of those times that either carried columns by Jyotirao Phule or propagated his work and philosophy. In 1875, Phule started *Deenbandhu*, which served as a voice for his Satyashodhak Samaj.

Preserved copies of these newspapers or references to them in books are the reason why we could put this book together. We present five key publications here.

1. **Gnyanoday:** The first copy of this bilingual newspaper was printed in 1842 at Ahmednagar. Henry Valentine was the first editor of *Gnyanoday*. It started as a fortnightly and later became a weekly magazine. Shahurao Kukde was the Marathi editor. Dedicated to the propagation of Christianity, it published a few letters and articles by Mahatma Phule and gave readers information about Phule's work from time to time.
2. **Shubh Vartaman Darshak:** The magazine started publishing under editor Canon Taylor from Kolhapur in both Marathi and English and survived till 1876. It praised Jyotirao Phule's book *Gulamgiri* and recognized him as one of the important social reformers to emerge from India.
3. **Satyadipika (the Lamp of Truth):** This magazine was started by Baba Padmanji[158] in 1861. It published several of Mahatma Phule's powadas—'*Vidyakhatyatil Bhrahman Pantoji*', '*Chhatrapati Shivaji Raje Bhosale*' and '*Brahminanche Kasab*'.

158 Baba Padmanji converted to Christianity and published several Christian journals during his lifetime such as *Prabhodaya*, *Ubhayadeepika*, *Satyavadi*, *Kutumbamitra* and *Ejapradarshak Patrika*.

4. **Prabhakar:** Started by Bal Shastri Jambhekar[159] and edited by Bhau Mahajan (real name Govind Vitthal Kunte), the first issue appeared in October 1841. It was published every Sunday. The *Prabhakar* formed an important base for the spread of reform in Maharashtra in the nineteenth century. The main feature of the *Prabhakar* were the '*Shata Patras*'[160] published in it. These letters were written by Gopal Hari Deshmukh, alias Lokhithavadi. This weekly was discontinued in 1865.
5. **Gnyanprakash:** This newspaper was started in 1849 by Krishnaji Trimbak Ranade. It began as a weekly, then became a biweekly and then a daily from 1904. Till 1862, it was lithographed and thereafter, it was printed. It chronicled Jyotirao Phule's work and views.

Another important voice of the time was Krishnashastri Chitpawan (1824–1876), born in Nasik in a Chitpavan Brahmin family.[161] This is significant because he was an outspoken critic[162] of Phule and was 'probably associated with the Dakshina Prize Committee when Phule's manuscript was rejected in 1855,

159 Bal Shastri Jambhekar was also the editor of the first Anglo-Marathi paper, *Bombay Darpan*, which started in 1832.

160 'Shatpatras' were written by Gopal Hari Deshmukh (Lokhitwadi). He wrote about the social issues like child marriage, caste system, widow remarriage, dowry system, and polygamy. He promoted women's emancipation and education of women.

161 Krishnashastri Chiplunkar was a social activist and Marathi writer from Maharashtra. For some years, he served as principal of the Teachers' Training College in Pune. Chiplunkar was a scholar especially in Sanskrit Nyaya, Dharma and Artha.

162 Veena Naregal, *Language, Politics, Elites and the Public Sphere: Western India Under Colonialism*, (Anthem Publishers, 2002).

but he supported Phule's initiatives in starting schools for lower caste communities'. Chiplunkar aggressively condemned Phule's evaluation of Brahminical hegemony, characterizing Phule 'as shamelessly bark(ing) away at Brahmins, and (vying) for crumbs that might be thrown at them according to the convenience of those in power'.[163] However, he supported Phule's initiative of opening schools for lower-caste communities.

163 Shefali Chandra, *The Sexual Life of English: Languages of Caste and Desire in Colonial India*, (Duke University Press, 2012). The author examines how the English language was used by nationalists to shape receptive audiences and creatively redeploy colonial concerns, and cites the above example.

Annexure 10

Given below is a list of texts that will help the reader better understand what is mentioned in the narrative. These works are not annotated in the text. However, they can help one delve further into a specific subject matter.

1. Margrit Pernau, translated by Joy Titheridge, *Ashraf into Middle Classes: Muslims in Nineteenth-Century Delhi*, Oxford University Press, 2013.
2. Santosh Kumar Rai (Assistant Professor, Department of History, SGTB Khalsa College, University of Delhi), 'The Fuzzy Boundaries: Julaha Weavers' Identity Formation in Early Twentieth Century United Provinces,' May 2013.
3. Professor Gopu Sudhakar, *Savitribai Phule: Pioneer of Women Empowerment*, Avni Publications, 2018.
4. A.B. Dharmadhikari (ed), *Maharashtratil Samaj Sudharak*, Chanakya Mandal, 2017.

5. Suhas Kulkarni and Milind Champanekar (eds), *Yani Ghadavala Sahastrak*, Rohan Prakashan.
6. J Natarajan, *History of Indian Journalism*, Publications Division, Ministry of Information & Broadcasting, 1995.
7. Ganesh Raut and Jyoti Raut, *Maharashtratil Parivartanacha Itihas* (1818–1960), Diamond Publications, 2011.
8. Hari Narke (ed), *Mahatma Phule Samagra Vangmay*, Maharashtra Government publication, 2020.
9. Ravinder Kumar, *Western India in the 19th century: A study in the social history of Maharashtra.*
10. Dr Shamshuddin Thamboli, 'Sathyasodhak Fathima', *Muslim Sathyasodhak Patrika*, July-August 2020, Poona.
11. Dadabhai Naoroji, *Poverty and Un-British Rule in India*, Publications Division, Ministry of Information and Broadcasting Government of India. Originally published in 1901 by Swan Sonnenschein and Company, London.
12. Tapan Raychaudhuri, Dharma Kumar, Meghnad Desai, Irfan Habib (eds.), *The Cambridge Economic History of India: Volume 2, c.1751-c.1970*, (Reprinted ed.). Cambridge University Press, 1983.
13. 'A report of the Female Schools in Poona from the Educational Inspector, Deccan Division', Bombay Public Consultations, General Department, 12 April 1856, no. 670 of 1856.
14. S.G. Malshe and Nanda Apte, *Vidhwa Vivah Chalwal (1800-1900)*, Mumbai: Stri Samshodhan Kendra, Shri Nathibhai Damodar Thakarsi Mahila Vidyapith, 1978.
15. P.G. Sahasrabudhe (ed), *Lokahitvadinchi Shatapatre*, Pune: Continental Prakashan, 1985.
16. S. Natarajan, *A Century of Social Reform in India*, Mumbai: Asia Publishing House, 1959.
17. Notes on India, Booklet #3 of the *India Reform*, London: Saunders & Stanford.

18. G.R. Gleig, *The Life of Major General Sir Thomas Munro* (3 volumes), 1840.
19. M. Taylor, *A Student's Manual of Indian History*, 1870.
20. Charles Trevelyan, *On the Education of the People of India*, 1838.

About the Author

Reeta Ramamurthy Gupta is a a bestselling author and a reviewer for Network18. She is an active proponent of the philosophy that the right mindset can help people re-script their lives and that of others. She is credited with the acclaimed Red Dot Experiment, a ten-year-long six-nation study on how culture impacts communication. A polyglot, she speaks five languages.

30 Years *of*

HarperCollins *Publishers* India

At HarperCollins, we believe in telling the best stories and finding the widest possible readership for our books in every format possible. We started publishing 30 years ago; a great deal has changed since then, but what has remained constant is the passion with which our authors write their books, the love with which readers receive them, and the sheer joy and excitement that we as publishers feel in being a part of the publishing process.

Over the years, we've had the pleasure of publishing some of the finest writing from the subcontinent and around the world, and some of the biggest bestsellers in India's publishing history. Our books and authors have won a phenomenal range of awards, and we ourselves have been named Publisher of the Year the greatest number of times. But nothing has meant more to us than the fact that millions of people have read the books we published, and somewhere, a book of ours might have made a difference.

As we step into our fourth decade, we go back to that one word – a word which has been a driving force for us all these years.

Read.

Harper Collins · 4th · HARPER PERENNIAL · HARPER BUSINESS · HARPER BLACK · हार्पर हिन्दी

HarperCollins *Children's Books* · HARPER DESIGN · HARPER VANTAGE · Harper Sport